SPIRITS DO RETURN

Mrs. Ida Belle White and Mark Twain

Originally Published in 1915

To him who has been my guide and inspiration; whose experience and talent have enabled me to be of assistance to those who are seeking the light, "Mark Twain," I dedicate this book.

TABLE OF CONTENTS

CHAPTER I

The Place of Trouble—The Convict's Story

CHAPTER II

Prison Life—Mysterious Influences

CHAPTER III

The Ghost of a Woman

CHAPTER IV

Accused of Murder

CHAPTER V

Official Excitement

CHAPTER VI

Discharged from the Hospital

CHAPTER VII

"My Brother a Convict!"

CHAPTER VIII

The Brother Sentenced to Hard Labor

CHAPTER IX

The Superintendent Tries to Solve the Mystery

CHAPTER X

Pat Allows the Prisoner to Escape

CHAPTER XI

The Mystery Deepens

CHAPTER XII

Another Dead Man

CHAPTER XIII

An Attempt to Bribe the Prisoner

CHAPTER XIV

The Convict's Prayer

CHAPTER XV

"Thank God, He Is Innocent!"

CHAPTER XVI

A New Prisoner in Cell No. 78

CHAPTER XVII

Deserted

CHAPTER XVIII

Pat's Temptation

CHAPTER XIX

A Clear Conscience Better than Money

CHAPTER XX

The Murderer Arrives

CHAPTER XXI

Remorse

CHAPTER XXII

Pat's Testimony

CHAPTER XXIII

Prayer-Meeting in Prison

INTRODUCTION

This book was written through the inspirational spirit of the well-known writer, Samuel L. Clemens—"Mark Twain." As I have never before written a book, the reader will see that I have had help from an unseen force—from the Spirit World.

I was told through a trumpet seance meeting, in the spirit voice of "Mark Twain," to get the materials and he would write me a book—or, rather, that he would inspire me and I could write it, but he would give me the words to write, which he has done.

I was not in an unconscious condition. I can turn from my writing and converse as if I had not been at work through the power of my guide. I can give abundance of proof of this statement, also for the statement made in the seance meeting by the spirit from Heaven.

"Mark Twain" has given me encouragement from time to time in regard to my book, and he has promised to write many more for me.

Ida Belle White.
(*Mrs. J. L. White.*)

CHAPTER I
The Place of Trouble—The Convict's Story

I passed by the house and within I heard a noise. I stopped and listened, and I heard screams. The voice sounded like that of a lady whom I once knew. I was puzzled to know what to do, but finally decided to enter. To my surprise, I did know the lady. I apologized for intruding, saying that I was attracted by the terrible screams and thought I recognized the voice.

The lady replied: "You are very kind, but I think I shall be able to settle my trouble without your help."

"I am very sorry, dear madam; I meant well," I said.

I took my departure, yet I felt that I should not have done so under the circumstances, for I knew that the talk the dear lady made was through fear, as the master over her was standing near.

I was greatly depressed, because of the way in which I had left the place of trouble. I had gone only a short distance when I decided to return. I did so, and, to my surprise, I found the dear lady dead, as it is called.

I was horrified. The brute had fled. What was I to do? Go also and leave the poor dead woman? I decided to do so. When at some distance from the scene, I was hailed and confronted by the real murderer and an officer, who accused me of the terrible crime.

What could I do? I knew that I was not guilty, but I failed to make the officer believe it.

I was taken to jail because of the crime committed by the one who had me arrested. But I had been seen coming from the house and I had dropped my handkerchief while wiping the tears from my eyes.

It was thought to be a plain case with convincing proof—of circumstantial evidence. Thrown in jail, I was at a loss to know what to do. I was not guilty, but to prove it was the next thing, and the most important thing to do. I hailed the turnkey as he passed, and asked for an attorney. I was favored with the services of one. I did some good thinking as to how I should prove my innocence.

"Well, my friend," said the attorney, "I have come to see what I can do for you. I see you need help. You do not look like a very bad man or a criminal."

"I thank you, sir," I replied. "I am not either, but why am I accused of murder?"

"Murder! You a murderer? Oh, no, I hope not!"

"I am not, but how shall I make the court understand that I am innocent?"

"Well, my friend, explain your case."

I explained matters, and he remarked: "I do not see how the court could find an innocent man like you guilty. I am going to show the court without trouble that you are not guilty. Have courage; I shall get you out of here as soon as possible."

The day of the trial was at hand. I had become haggard and worn from the terrible strain, from the uncomfortable cell which I had occupied. My case was called. All ready, I was told to take my oath, and then I was sworn to tell the truth and nothing but the truth. If I could make the court understand that I was innocent, I would soon be a free man.

"Will you tell the court all about this case?" said my attorney.

I proceeded to do so, but, to my horror, I was proved guilty to the jury and sentenced by the judge.

What was I to do? I went back to jail to wait for a new trial. If that failed, it meant ten years in prison at hard work. I had been convicted on circumstantial evidence; my handkerchief being found in the house of the murdered woman. I tried to console myself with the belief that in some way I would be helped out.

I had remained in jail three months when one night I was thinking of the advice my poor old mother had given me, and that was: "When in trouble, pray, pray, pray!" I began to pray, and as I prayed I felt encouraged. After that, I prayed often, hoping that my prayers would be answered. At last I could see that I was fortunate to know within that I was not the real murderer; then I thought that I should pray for the murderer, and I did pray as I never prayed before.

Oh, what a terrible thing it is to be accused of a crime so great as that and be innocent!

A new trial was denied me. What was I to do? God knows I was innocent, but I could not make men believe so here on this earth. The day for the journey to the penitentiary was at hand, and I must go for another's crime.

As the turnkey called us from our little, dark cells he said: "Please get ready, for we will have to take the morning train to your home—for some of you a home for some time to come."

That included me; that meant a home for ten years—and innocent! I had no appetite that morning, for I was thinking of the injustice done to many innocent men, and I was one of them.

We were locked together—shackled—and started away to prison. On arrival we were listed for different crimes. A murderer, numbered 78! And the worst, I thought, was when they cut and shaved my head of hair. Then I was told to don my new suit of stripes and checks. That alone was enough to make any man falter.

"This way," I heard a gruff voice say.

I looked for someone to look and in a second, I felt the strong arm.

"To you I am speaking. I want to show you your cell."

I had not recovered from the shock of my garments. I was shoved headlong into my cell, dark, and oh, so dreary! Anyone who could experience my feelings at that moment would never commit a crime.

I can not say that I rested well on my new bed that night. I thought that morning would never come. Yet I do not know why I should have longed for day, as I had so long a time to stay. At last breakfast was served—or, rather, thrown at us. I was feverish and excited. All the time I wondered what my work would be. I did not have to wonder long. I was unlocked from my cell and told to step out and fall in line. I did so and onward we marched. A halt was called and I was told to step aside.

A very important man, called guard, said: "You are wanted here, sir!"

I stepped aside and was shown my work, which was hard, even harder than anything I had ever done. I was told to pick up the sledge and was shown in what shape to hammer the iron.

I hesitated, and finally said: "My God! man, I never did such hard work, and I don't think I can do this."

All the sympathy I received was: "You do the work or you will be thrown into a dark dungeon to decide if you can, and you will get bread and water until you do decide."

I thought that I would as soon go into a dungeon as to work myself to death. However, I changed my mind and picked up the sledge, but I had not strength to wield it.

I fell upon my knees and prayed that God would give me help. While I was praying the guard came up and with his monstrous club gave me one blow, knocking me senseless.

I cried out as I came to my senses: "Man alive, do not strike me again! Can you not see I am not strong enough to do that work?"

"Oh! you fellows all have the same old gag to tell. Not strong enough! Ha, ha! But you are strong enough to strangle a poor woman to death."

I rose to my feet, and shouted: "I am an innocent man! I will be proven so before I leave this prison."

"All who are sent here are innocent. Some of you surely get justice in trials."

"I did not, for I was sentenced on circumstantial evidence, and I know and my God knows that I am innocent! The dear woman who was murdered knows who killed her."

"Well, the woman is dead, and you can not prove by her that you did not kill her."

"My friend, she is not dead. Her body is, but her spirit is not, and she can and will come and let it be known who the real murderer is."

"Here, if you are crazy, we will put you in the mad-house. I know when you are dead you are dead."

"I hope to be able to convince you before I leave here that the body dies, but the spirit lives on and returns and will and can talk."

"Here, are you going to work? I have heard enough of your foolish talk."

"I will try, sir."

No one can realize how I suffered. I was not able to work, yet I was forced to do so. I worried through that day. I could not eat the poor food that was given us. Another morning came. During the restless night I had prayed for help from the Spirit World, and I felt that my prayers were answered.

The guard called: "You, I say, that never dies, get out here and get your breakfast and go to work."

I stood up, and said: "I am ready, sir, but this morning I am so sick."

"You eat what you get, and in a hurry too, for we want to see you at work."

I obeyed, and was soon on the road to work.

The prison laws were that we were not allowed to speak to our fellow-men. I watched my chance to speak, and when opportunity presented, I said:

"Friend, how long are you here for?"

He did not answer. I thought perhaps he was hard of hearing, and repeated the words. He finally looked up and moved his lips. I knew he had served some time, as he had learned the sight movement of the lips, and I did not and could not understand that. I saw that I was lost, not knowing how to talk in that way.

The guard said roughly: "You are not doing much. Here, are you watching for opportunity to lay down on me when I am not looking?"

"I am not, guard. I am doing all I am able to."

"I think if you had a day or two rest in the rest-room it would help you. Come along here with me."

The rest-room was a dungeon, dark as night. When I heard the heavy iron door close after me, I fell upon my knees and prayed God to take me from the place of darkness. I was hungry and cold. All the time I could hear the words:

"We know you are innocent and will help you, and you shall be out of this place of unjust punishment."

That night—oh, so long! Cold and hungry I was—I had no bed. The following morning, I was given water and was told to drink and be merry; yes, to be *merry*! I wonder if the outside world could and does believe the stories of the unfortunate ones who, guilty or not guilty, have to endure tortures behind prison walls.

I remained there three days and grew weaker all the time. Why should I not grow weak, living on water and darkness and standing up to sleep?

I was put to work at the same hard labor which I had performed before. I grew faint and fell at my post. I lay there when the guard came upon me. How he did swear! He clubbed me to my feet and reached out for me. One jerk from him raised me from my feet. He had subsisted upon good, substantial food. I was weak, hungry, and sick.

I was taken to the office for a talk on "the carpet," as we called it in prison. As the Power over all men seemed to look down on me, I raised my eyes to Heaven and asked for proof to convince the official that I was an innocent man. I was hoping against hope for proof, and I heard a voice say: "Take him out. I will see what this lady wants." The official saw one whom neither the guard nor I saw. I was led away, back to the dungeon.

Some hours afterwards I was again taken to "the carpet." I was praying silently for proof of my innocence. Again, I was told: "Step aside, for the ladies come first." Later I was told of a very mysterious lady who showed herself unannounced and when she was spoken to, vanished.

Who could it be? When I was a child, I often sat with my dear father and mother around the fireplace and listened with the cold chills running down my back to stories of ghosts, as they called them, and how the ghosts would come and go. No, not where I sat in my dark dungeon and wondered if that lady could talk, and, if so, why could she not come to me and talk to me, as I was all alone. And I again thought perhaps I would not care to have her come to me—not as long as I was in the dark and all alone. But what and who could the mysterious lady be? I was so interested in our ghost woman that I forgot my own troubles.

That night, as I was wishing and praying for morning, and wondering what would be done with me on "the carpet," I felt that I could hardly wait. At last the sun shone on the prison walls once more, and I was heartily glad. One more day less of my ten years served. But there were still years to serve, and with such treatment and hard labor there was not much encouragement for a poor convict.

I heard my cell door open. A gruff voice called to me to step out. I was glad to do so, and was told to come along.

CHAPTER II
Prison Life—Mysterious Influences

As I was taken through the iron doors, I heard a slam after me. The guard also heard the same noise. Turning, he called to me to halt, saying: "What was that?"

"I'm sure, I do not know, sir," I replied; "I only heard a noise."

"I am not sure whether I did or not. I thought I saw a lady, as I turned my head."

"Could it be a ghost?" I thought, and, if so, why was it following me?

"Guard, what is the complaint against this man?" inquired the superintendent.

"He will not work, sir."

"Not work? Oh! Well, you have had a taste of the dungeon, have you not? If that will not do, we shall have to try some other means to get you to work, and that will be to tie your hands above your head until you are willing to work. How do you think you would like that?"

"I am willing to work if I had lighter work," I said; "I have never had to do such heavy work, and I am unable to do it."

"Take him out," commanded the superintendent, "and put him on the rack, and when you feel you can do the work, we will be glad to take you to your work."

I did not know what "the rack" meant and was very willing to follow. To my horror, it was a place where my hands were tied above my head. I stood facing the wall. Imagine the punishment of one fellow-man upon another! I begged for mercy. All my pleadings were ignored. When the guard had finished tying my hands, I was told that he would be around inside of twenty-four hours, to see if I had changed my mind.

I knew that I could not stand the punishment long. I began to pray. I prayed for dear old mother to come to her helpless and innocent son. I began to feel the rack quiver. I was startled. I ceased praying for a moment. I thought I could feel the clasps move on my wrists. I was shaken with fear. Was I going mad, or did I feel the clasps move? To my great surprise, I was lowered so I could stand on the bottoms of my feet; before I could touch only the floor with my toes. I felt a terrible feeling come over me and all was dark. When I came to myself, I was released. Could the guard have knocked me senseless? How was I loosened? I did not see him near me. I did not feel hurt from any blow. What could have happened to me! I remained there in a wonderment of thought as to what could have happened. About five hours had passed when I heard footsteps and the guard entered. He was astonished when he saw that I was loosed.

"What does this mean?" he exclaimed.

"I am not able to say, sir. Did you not free my hands?"

"I? No, sir; you know that I did not, and who did?"

"I do not know. I was praying to my dear old mother, who died many years ago, to come to me and help me, as I was innocent of the crime for which I am being punished, and while I was praying I felt a dizziness come over me, and my hands were loosened and I was thrown to the floor, and when I came to my senses, I was free."

"So, you think that story will go here, do you? Well, come along. We shall see if we can tie you so your prayers will not untie you."

"My God! do not punish me any more seriously. I am not deserving of this. I say to you that I am innocent."

"We would have no use for the building if all of you fellows could prove to the world that you were innocent. If you are not guilty, why have you been brought here? Surely you had some justice done you."

"Sir, I was convicted on circumstantial evidence. I was not proved guilty, for I am not guilty. The guilty one is at large, and the innocent one is here for ten years."

"You are having your own way about this argument. I only know you are here for murder, and it is my duty to see that you are working for the next ten years. Come along with me."

I was taken to "the carpet" and the look of the officer and higher official was like daggers. I trembled from head to foot.

"You here again? What is the trouble, guard?"

"I found this man standing with hands untied when I entered the rack."

"What does this mean? Who untied you?"

I saluted the superintendent, and replied: "I do not know."

"Well, we will see if we can find out. Take him back and double-tie his hands. Strap his feet also, and tip-toe him, and perhaps he will be willing to work by and by."

I began to beg. How could anyone punish his brother man so? I said:

"I am human and have feeling. I do not deserve such hard treatment. I would work willingly if you would give me work that I can do. I can not do hard labor—I never did."

"You will do what we see fit to give you to do, and if you are not willing, you go back to the rack."

I could not stand the ordeal. On bended knees I begged for mercy, and the mercy shown me was a clubbing, and I was marched back to the rack.

"Now, sir, I will strap you, as I was ordered to do, and I will be around, perhaps, to see the other fellow untie you."

As before, I was strapped with uplifted hands, and drawn from the floor to the tips of my toes. I was exhausted with fear, and as I was being tied, both feet together, I cried out: "God, have pity! Give me help and strength to stand this, for Thou, O Heavenly Father, dost know that I am innocent."

I heard the heavy iron door close behind me, as I thought, for the last time. I could not see how I could ever withstand this punishment.

Suddenly I began to experience the peculiar feeling of dizziness that had come over me before. I felt my hands being loosened, then I knew nothing more. I lay I do not know how long. The first I remembered was when I again heard the door slam and over me stood the guard and the superintendent. I was told to get up. I obeyed, and the look on the faces of those men I shall never forget.

After I was questioned as to how I felt, the dizziness began again to come upon me. I was again taken back to "the carpet," but this time with more of the feeling of sympathy than before.

"I am at a loss, sir, to know what to do with you," said the superintendent. "I think that I shall have an investigation of your case and see if we can find why and what power you have, if any. I was an eye-witness to your being untied this time, and no one assisted. Invisible power is the only explanation I can make."

Again, I was taken back, but not to the rack—to my cell, where I was given some coffee, and kind words with it. I was wondering what this meant when I heard footsteps, then voices saying:

"Let them tie you as often as they will. I shall free you. You are innocent, and shall not be punished."

I looked for the one whose voice I heard, and, to my surprise, could not see anyone. I shuddered. I did not understand this.

I had drunk my coffee, and was feeling somewhat better from its effect and that of the kind words, when the superintendent entered with others.

As I arose to greet them, I was drawn back by some invisible power. Remaining seated, I was told to arise. I could not do so, and replied that I could not.

One of the gentlemen seized my arm and told me to stand up. I tried to do so, and could not. I was taken hold of by another and told to stand, but again I could not. Then they tried to lift me up, and they could not move me.

I became alarmed. I did not feel ill—only slightly dizzy.

They debated as to what they should do about my case. I could not understand such a mystery. I only knew that I was freed, by whom I could not tell.

The mystery was growing in my mind. As I was sent for by the doctor, whom they called in to diagnose my case, I arose without effort, to the surprise of the guard, and walked unassisted to the office. There I confronted the doctor, apparently a well man, on my feet, and feeling well anyway.

I was thoroughly examined, and pronounced physically well. Once more I was taken back to "the carpet," and was told that I would be given lighter work, and to try not to be subject to any such treatment hereafter, as disobedient prisoners have to be compelled to work.

I was taken to the library, and told to book out all literature, as called for. I became very much interested in the work and was trying to make the best of it. I thought: "I am going to see if I can find some literature in here which will comfort me and help me to pass this long time which I must spend inside of these prison walls."

I had an order for a book called "The Ghost of a Woman." Ghost of a woman! I wondered if the prisoner who ordered it had seen the ghost of this woman talked of in this place and hoped to find a book telling what her mission is here, I thought: "I too should like to know."

As I was tracing along the line of literature, I was confronted with a book entitled "The Wisdom." What could that be? We all needed some of that, I especially. If I had had more, I would not be here. "As it is, I am here," I thought, "and I am willing to find wisdom."

I laid the book aside to take along with me to my cell to read when I should have the opportunity. I then continued the search for "The Ghost of a Woman."

As the guard entered, he said: "Well, you are not making much headway getting out those orders."

"I have an order here for a book entitled 'The Ghost of a Woman.'"

"Here, we have a real live ghost, in here, of a woman, and that is enough ghost. Let me see who has left that crazy order. What! The superintendent wants this book. Well, look it up. I guess he has not had enough, but I have. I do not have to read of her, for I see her times enough."

I was left to continue the search for the ghost book. At last I found a similar title and laid the book aside. I would perhaps find the desired book in my search for other literature.

All orders filled; I began to deliver to each prisoner's cell. We were allowed light to read by, two hours each night. I passed these two hours much more pleasantly with my book of wisdom than I could have done otherwise. Did I find wisdom? Do we all find it when we need it most? Some of us do not. It was so in my case. I got my wisdom after I could do no good with it, only to look forward ten years.

CHAPTER III
The Ghost of a Woman

I was told on the following morning, by the guard, that I would have to leave the library and do some printing.

"Printing! Dear sakes alive, man, I am no printer!" I exclaimed.

"Those are the orders," he replied. "Obey your orders."

"I am very willing to do so if I knew how," I said.

"I see that you have been reading a book, here, called 'Wisdom.' You should be able to do something."

"If I had all the wisdom in my head that is in that book, I should not be here."

"You are debating the question too long. Come along here, sir."

I was taken to the printing quarters and given instructions as to what to do. To my surprise, the part to which I was assigned I could very easily handle. A prisoner said:

"I am here to give you instructions how to prepare what we call '*The Daily Press*'—news, something for the prisoners to read, that they may know what goes on inside these walls that will be of benefit to them. We have some good men here. They are not all criminals because sent here. Some from misfortune, others from circumstantial evidence, which later is proven. I am always glad to see an innocent man found so. I am speaking in behalf of myself, here for another's crime. To make the best of it is all that I can do, as do many others, who are here as innocent as I am."

I could not speak. I felt as if I were choking with sympathy for that poor chap. I too was serving a sentence for another's crime. I am not sure but that his number was on the order for a book entitled "I Am Innocent of Crime," a book to be found on the shelves of the prison library.

I felt that I could work by the side of this fellow-man—this prisoner—more cheerfully, as he had authority to talk so as to be able to give instructions to inexperienced help.

I was told to prepare an article for *The Press*, on how to use power to control yourself as well as others. I was very willing to do what I could. That is all anyone can do—the best we can.

I have been in the presence of men to whom I could not talk as freely as I should like to, and in the presence of others to whom I could talk fast enough. Those to whom one can not talk freely have a higher power over one, and those to whom one can talk freely are the persons over whom one has power. Who has not had the power experience? When we come in touch with those with whom we can not talk freely, it is power over each other. I am leading out to the power we can not resist. What is that? I am able to say that I could not resist going into that house where a crime was committed to see what the trouble was with the poor lady who was murdered—murdered, and I accused of the crime!

I was wondering what my fellow-man under whose instructions I was placed was there for, and I became so deep in thought that I was spoken to by him:

"Well, you must have your work done for *The Press*, and time for the press to start is soon at hand."

"I was so deep in thought I forgot myself, sir. I beg your pardon. I will try not to let that happen again."

At that moment the guard stepped in. I was accosted in such a brutal way that my fellow-prisoner interceded for me and asked the guard to have mercy on me.

"I am quite sure that the man will do all he can," he said.

"Yes, he will when he is driven to it. He has caused us trouble from the day he landed here."

"I am sorry, guard. If I could have complied with your rules and work, I should have been glad to do so; but I was not able to do the hard labor you asked me to do."

"Was it hard work to strangle a poor woman to death? You found that a very easy job, did you not?"

"Man, I can not stand it to be accused of a crime I did not commit!" At that moment I gave way to my feelings and cried out: "O Father in Heaven, can not I prove my innocence?"

I found myself lying on my cot when revived. I knew not what had happened. I could remember the conversation and nothing more after that until the present time.

I was in a dazed condition and had the feeling that someone was near and could see me. I was taken back to the printer's shop, and must say that the instructor seemed to have a cold feeling for me. I said:

"I notice that you are not quite so friendly as before. Have I offended you?"

"I have no use for a murderer, sir, and especially for one who murders a helpless woman."

"I say to you, kind fellow-prisoner, that I am innocent."

"Yes. I have your reputation from the guard. Now, you get to hard work here, and no more of your pleading innocence."

"I am going to do all that I can, sir, and as well as I can, to please you."

I continued to prepare the press work. I wrote of the way to live and live right. We all make mistakes. Some repent, others never do. Who has not made mistakes which he would, if he could, undo? I wrote:

"O dear fellow-prisoners, we have all made mistakes. If we had not, we would not be here."

As those words were for *The Press*, the prisoner's daily paper, I thought them very appropriate. As I left for lunch, I noticed the man who was so indifferent before. He stopped to see what my subject was. I could not help but see a change in his manner toward me; he acted in a more brotherly way.

As I was locked in for the night, I was tired and sick—heart-sick. I could not see, for the life of me, how I could stand many years of prison life. At last I closed my eyes for the night—a long, dark, dreaming one. When a child I ofttimes sat at my mother's knee, before I was sent to bed, and was taught my prayers; to ask Our

Father in Heaven to watch over me. The next day I knelt and prayed as I had long years ago for my dear old mother, and asked God to help me the following day.

Somehow, I felt better after I prayed. Eight o'clock was the hour for work to begin, and I was somewhat encouraged that morning. I knew not why. Perhaps the kindness which was shown me by my fellow-prisoner the day before was what lightened my heart.

The day's work had begun when I was spoken to by a gruff voice, and told that I was wanted at the office.

My heart was crushed. I thought perhaps I was to undergo some painful ordeal, as heretofore. I could not keep up courage to get to the office. I was trembling with fear when I entered. I did not ask what I was wanted for. I felt that I should know soon enough.

Suddenly the officer looked up and smiled. I did not understand the meaning and remained silent. He then spoke as if I were a guest instead of a prisoner:

"Well, sir, I have some work for you to do. I want to find out who the lady is I see here and don't see here, although I hear her voice, and she seems to be calling your name. Do you or can you explain the mystery?"

At that moment I could not speak. After a few moments, I tried to answer in this way:

"I am not able to give any information whatever. I know not whom you see or hear."

"Well, sir, can you account for your mysterious freedom from the rack?"

"I am not able to do so."

"Neither can I, and I sat there and watched you being untied. Did you ever hear your dear old friends tell of ghosts?"

"I hear this is a ghost doing this."

"I am not able to say."

"Neither am I."

"Well, do you think you could find out if it were one?"

"I could not say."

"I am going to have you remain in this office a few days and see if you can see what I do. I am not going to have you do anything, only look and listen."

"Sir, I am not a coward, but I would prefer to work, as I am becoming used to hard labor and would like to keep busy."

"I think you will find this job hard enough, and it will keep you busy enough—or, at least, I have been pretty busy holding myself in here. I feel I need my vacation now."

What was I to do? I was trembling from head to foot, and looking on all sides of me for the ghost. Presently the door opened. I collapsed and was deathly faint, when I found it was only a man.

"I have made arrangements for the prisoner to remain here in the office with me. His place may be filled by another," said the officer to the man.

"I am glad to stay in here with you," I said. "What shall I do?" I trembled so that my voice quivered.

"Well, sir, I am going to let you take that comfortable chair and sit there for a time, while I am busy."

I was seated presently. I felt my chair move. I moved also, and I cried out: "I am going mad!" I was being moved in my chair.

"That is nothing, sir. You perhaps will be moved as often as I have been, and that is many times."

I knew not what to do. I could not disobey orders, but felt that I could no longer remain there. While debating whether to sit down or stand up, I was confronted by the form of a woman.

I fell back and cried out: "Mother! mother! mother!"

When I became able to speak again, I told that it was my dear old mother, and I was asked to describe her, which I did.

"Well, there are two ghosts here, then," said the officer; "for that is not the description of the one I saw."

Was I to go through with another experience of seeing another ghost? I fell on my knees and begged to be sent back to the printing shop.

"You are doing more good here than any place in which I have placed you. I think you have a good, long job here—or, at least, until we find out what the mysterious lady wants around here."

"I am glad to be with you, but you are not giving me any punishment of hard labor, as the judge said you should."

"Well, I don't know. Perhaps you have not worked at this long enough to find the hard part of it."

What should I say next to find some excuse to get away from there? I had thought of all excuses, and presently I began to feel sick, or pretended so. Oh, how I did moan! I did not create any sympathy. The officer informed me that he had to moan louder than that when they got after him.

I got well the next breath. What to try next I did not know. I could not break away from prison. Soon I heard footsteps. I looked, but could see no one. I asked the officer if he heard anything.

"Oh, yes, I hear them. You are not frightened, are you? Well, I have become used to them, and you will if you stay here a few days."

"Man, I will die if I have to remain in this office another day!"

"I have felt as you do, and I have had the same experience ever since you came to this prison. And your name is repeated many times a day. Can you explain what all this means?"

"I am an innocent man charged with murder done by another. I am not treated justly. That is all I can say or know. I do not know anything about these voices or mysterious women, but I am quite sure that I saw my dear old mother, as she was when living. I do not understand it. I am told that we never die. To explain further I am not able, but I do want to get out of this office. I feel strong enough to do any kind of hard work."

"Well, sir, I am glad that we have found a way to make you work, and you may go back to hard labor."

The guard was called and orders given to take the prisoner back to hard labor—not the printing shop, as he was willing to do hard work.

"You may try to lift some of those anvils which we have orders to ship. It requires three or four men to get them where we can load and ship."

Could I do what required the strength of three or four men?

"You may come along here."

As I was leaving for the shipping yards, I felt that I was accompanied by others beside my guard, but I could see no one. Presently we confronted the place of shipping, and I was shown what was to be done. I looked at the guard, and exclaimed:

"Man, do you expect me to load those heavy irons on the truck?"

"I do."

"Well, I do not think that your expectations will be granted. I am not a giant, and neither am I a myth. I am only a man, as you are."

"I did not bring you over here to argue that question. What you must do is do the best that you can and try to load up."

"I will not disobey orders, but I do not see or understand why I should be asked to do such hard work—why the work of two or three men should be placed on one."

Once more I felt that I could not get courage to try. I could hear someone say:

"We will help you."

I looked for someone, as before, but no one was near.

"Well, if you are going to work, do so at once."

I bent over to make an attempt to satisfy my guard. As I did so I received help, and behold, I could feel the iron move! I was horrified, but I saw that I was moving it along toward the truck, and that without strain or great effort on my part.

As the guard saw the great load moving, he called out: "You are moving it! Be careful, be careful!"

I could hear the sound of someone breathing heavily. I put the load down and turned to see if I had help. As I looked for the guard, to my surprise, he was lying on the floor near by. I stepped over and spoke to him. He did not answer. I called out to him to speak to me. No answer. The shipping space was off to itself, and at that moment there was no one near. I could not think what to do. I could see at once that I would be accused of harming or killing him, as he lay apparently dead.

CHAPTER IV
Accused of Murder

I thought of the other wrong accusation of murder. Now, perhaps, it would happen again. I finally decided to call for help. An officer stepped up. When he saw his fellow-officer lying as I have said, apparently dead, he at once accused me.

"What have you done to this man?"

"I am innocent of any harm to that man. I did not even see him fall."

"What were you doing that you did not see him fall?"

"I, sir, was doing what he told me to do—loading those pieces of iron on the truck. I heard deep breathing and turned to look, and found him as you see him now."

"Well, I do not believe one word you have told me, and more, no sane man would ask another to do what it would require three or four strong men to do."

"I was not only asked to do so, but I was doing it. I had moved the iron to the distance you see, from the remainder."

"Now you come along. I will send the hospital word about him."

Again, I was taken to the office. I wondered what would be done now. As I had no way of proving that I did not commit the deed, I could not make them understand that I had not harmed the guard.

The officer said: "I will tell you. I found the guard lying on the floor. I do not know if he is dead or in a faint. I do know that he looks very much like a dead man."

"What! Do you mean to tell me that this man has committed another murder?"

"I am not a murderer, and I did not harm this man. I did not, I say, and God is my judge."

"We shall have to take some unusual proceedings with you. I am sure that when we find out the truth, which I hope and pray to do, and we will if this man is not dead and he tells the story of how he was harmed, we will be able to at least see what and why so much mystery surrounds you."

"I hope he may live and be able to tell the story, for I am anxious to find out how he happened to be in the condition found."

"Are you quite sure that you do not already know?"

"I do not, sir."

"I am at a loss to know what to do with you and where next to place you. Do you think that you could prove to us that you did move the iron?"

"I do not know, sir. I am quite sure that it moved, and I did not see anyone near, and that is why I stopped when I heard the moaning—to see what was wrong, and I saw my guard lying on the floor."

"You tell a very plain story, but can we believe it? I can not, and will try you out again on the same work."

To the other guard he said: "You may take him back and see if what he has been telling is true."

"Oh! I beg you not to try my strength on what would require three times the amount of strength I have, and perhaps cause another circumstantial evidence of murder, if the guard should be found dead, after reaching the hospital."

"I shall not expect you to do so much. I want you to substantiate the story you are telling us. And now you may go back to the shipping quarters."

I was taken, this time accompanied by the officer to whom I was talking and who was giving orders to place me where I should be given the work.

I thought, on the way back, that I should fall with fear and weakness. I could not see how I could have courage to try to move the unreasonable load again.

We are shown no mercy in prison—at least, I was not. Instead, I was bidden to do work which it was impossible for me to do, outside of prison walls. We accomplish a great many feats through fear. I am sure that I could not accomplish many which I did except through fear.

"Now, sir," said the officer, "you say that you moved that iron that distance?"

"I did, sir."

"Well, you may now show if you can move it as far, again, and I shall see that while you are moving it you do not move me too, as you did the other, to the hospital."

At that moment I could not speak. Instead I could hear someone speak to me, and the words were:

"I will help you. Take hold."

I did so. As I bent over, I could see several trying to get hold of the anvils. I felt that my strength was greater than ever before, and I could see the anvils move along, apparently with ease. After I had moved them to where we wished them to be, I raised up and found that I was all alone. I looked around for the officer and guard, but they were not to be seen.

As I was standing meditating as to what I should do, a prisoner all alone with no guard in sight, I wondered if I should call for a guard, or try to move another mass of iron.

At that moment a voice called to me. Turning to look, I was confronted by a new guard, whom I had never before seen. We could readily tell the guards by their uniforms.

"How does it come," he said, "that you are outside of your rank and here doing nothing with no guard near?"

"Sir, I am here working and had a guard with me."

"Well, where is he now?"

"I do not know, sir. While I was lifting these anvils and placing them where we could load them for shipment, he disappeared."

"Go on! What are you giving me? You alone lifting these anvils?"

"Yes, sir."

"Do you know that you are not strong enough to lift one end of any one of them, not even the smallest-sized one there?"

"Well, I do not understand, myself, how I did it, but I did."

"I think that I shall have to take you to 'the carpet.' You are astray from work in some part of this prison."

Dear, oh, dear! Back to "the carpet"! On the way I could hear a hearty laughing, and I felt that I was being ridiculed by my fellow-men, because I was taken so often to the so-called "carpet." As we knew, usually when an officer was taking a prisoner to the office many times, he was sent for as a punishment for disobeying. In another moment I thought I could not have heard the prisoners laugh, as that was against the rules. Then what did I hear?

We at last reached the office, only to find the superintendent gone, the door locked, and no way of getting in, as the door of the office leads inside of the prison walls. Therefore, it is necessary to have locked doors at all times.

The next thing to do with me was to lock me in my cell, as I could not make the officer believe that I was working when he found me.

After some time in my cell I was again sent for, this time by a new guard, and was told to go to the office with him.

As we entered, I saw several men whom I had never before seen in the office. I noticed that they were officers of the prison. They seemed to be very much excited, and I must say that I too was excited. I did not know what next they would or could do with me.

CHAPTER V
Official Excitement

I was told to be seated. As I turned to the empty chair I was not permitted to sit down. I could not do so. I tried as hard as I could, but I did not move. Again, I was spoken to, and told to be seated. This time the voice that commanded me to be seated was gruff and harsh.

I replied: "I am trying to, sir, but I can not move."

"You sit down. We are going to find out what is wrong with you. I have called in all the higher officers, and we intend to have your case thoroughly investigated this day."

All this time I did not move—I could not, and presently I heard a voice say:

"Do not sit down. We will not allow you to do so."

Suddenly I was seized by the officer, and was again told to sit down.

I said: "I would obey if I could, but I can not move."

"Well, I will move you."

I could see that the officer made an effort to compel me to move, and I could feel myself grow rigid. Presently I felt myself begin to move toward the door of the inside prison, and for a moment everything seemed dark. I felt a sickening feeling come over me. I began to lose consciousness, and found myself sitting on the chair against the prison door. All the officers were lying on the floor. I cried out for help.

"Come to my rescue!" I cried. "I have not harmed anyone here."

At that moment guards came from all directions, and shouted: "Open the door!" I could not and did not move.

Again, they shouted, and I did not move. I did not look like a dead man, sitting there, but I must frankly say that I felt like one, and if wishes could have been granted, would have been one, for I was in prison for one murder, perhaps two, and from the surroundings it might be several, as these men all looked like corpses to me.

Presently "Bang!" went the door. The guards had gotten great heavy irons and were trying to force the door open. When they succeeded, I was the first one to be taken care of. As a matter of fact, the dead men, as they thought them, could be gotten away in only one way, and that is carried. I could get away, but did not have a chance. But I got something else, a good beating from the officers.

Oh, how I did beg and try to explain to them that I had not harmed anyone! but in vain. I was laid up for some time from the severe treatment.

I knew not what became of the officials, or how badly, if at all, they were hurt. Neither did I know how it happened that they were all lying so helpless on the floor.

It was unfortunate for me, as they did not know of this mysterious power nor of the "lady ghost"—so called, nor of the unseen power which had put our friend in the hospital. He had recovered enough to take notice when the officers were brought into the hospital. He naturally inquired if there had been a prison raid, and the answer was:

"More serious than that. We would be glad to let some of our prisoners go if we could do so, as they seem to do much as they please with themselves and others too. The great mystery is causing much trouble, and we can not find out what is wrong."

"How long have I been here and why am I here? I am not hurt. I was not attacked by my prisoner. The last I remember I was cautioning him to be careful, as I saw him lifting what no three men could. That is my last recollection. I have not an ache nor a pain, and why am I here? Bring the prisoner to me."

"We can not. He is also in the hospital. He disobeyed so much that he received such treatment as to be sent to the hospital."

"He has! Tell me what has he done?"

"To the best of my knowledge, he has murdered five of the officials, all brought in here just now, as you have seen."

"Murdered! murdered! I want to get to him."

"You too have been injured by him, and you must remain quiet until pronounced out of danger."

"I am not injured, and he did not harm me. I must be taken to the office, that I may declare this man innocent of that crime."

"I shall have to have orders from your physician before I could consider taking you out of the hospital. I fear that you are not yourself, when you say that the prisoner did not harm you."

"I can swear before all, and by God in Heaven, that he did not. I must be taken to him and tell him that I will say that he did me no harm."

"You will have plenty of time to prove his innocence, and tell why you are here and how you did get hurt if he did not do it."

"I am not hurt. I am as well as I ever was in my life, and I must see the doctor and say to him that I must be out of here."

"Very well; I will go to the doctor and send him to you."

CHAPTER VI
Discharged from the Hospital

"Good morning, sir," said the doctor when he entered. "I was told that you wished to see me."

"If it is the rule of this hospital to be discharged by the doctor, then I want to see you. Outside of that I do not need you."

"Are you preparing to leave here?"

"I am. Why should I remain here? I am not sick."

"You are not able to leave. I see that you are in a very dangerous condition."

"Tell me why you say and think so."

"I am going to say to you that I have seen many such cases as yours—delirious. They do not feel ill and know not what is wrong, and think they are in the very best of health. I will take your temperature."

"One moment, please—"

"Temperature 104. You are a very sick man. You must remain in this ward."

"I must save the accused prisoner. He did not hurt me. I distinctly remember that I was saying to him, 'Be careful!' and he was not even looking toward me."

"Well, sir, I fear that you do not understand. I have been attending some of our officials who have been hurt very badly by the same prisoner, and we have him in the mad-house, very dangerously injured by the officer who found them a few minutes after the act had been committed, just as you were found, and he pleaded innocent, just as he did in your case."

"I will say to you, and I must say to all men, that he did not harm me. I am not ill. I must be discharged from this place."

"Very well; I will see about it."

Going to another part of the hospital, where the other patients who had fallen to the floor had been taken, the doctor, turning to the superintendent, said:

"Good morning. You are feeling much better this morning?"

"I am, sir. I do not feel ill. I am not ill, and shall leave for the office at once. Why am I here? I have not been ill. As I awakened this morning I could not for a moment realize where I was and what had happened."

"Have you no recollection of any trouble?"

"I do not remember of any. Oh, yes! The mysterious ghost is all the trouble I have had for some time. But how is the guard the prisoner hurt? Is he dead? What have they done with him? Did I not order him to be brought in, so that the superior officers might see what could be done? Oh, I do remember, now! It was not clear in my mind until now; now it has begun to clear up so that I can remember. Pray tell me why you brought me here? I do not remember of coming. Who is in charge of the office?"

"An officer is taking care of the office. It is well cared for.

"I have some mail here. Shall I leave it at the office, or here?"

"The officer is able to read."

"You are not to make me sick by saying these things. I am not sick.

"What have I here? A letter from the murderer of the mysterious woman ghost! What does this mean? Listen:

"'I want to confess. I did the murdering, and not the prisoner you have there. He is innocent.'

"Well, well! He does not give his name and I wonder how he knows of a mysterious ghost, as I have guarded very carefully about the mystery. I have avoided gossip about the matter, preferring that it should not get out. But I should be glad to free the ghost and let her out. I should be entirely willing if she would go. When I go to the office, I shall send for the prisoner whose name I hear called so much. And I shall show him this letter and notice if any change comes over him.

"Now I shall leave for the office, and you, guard, may bring the prisoner numbered 78 there."

Soon a guard appeared at my side, saying: "You are wanted at the office. Get up there."

"I am not able to go. I have been badly hurt, and I am heart-sick. I know that I can not live this life any longer."

"You will not have to, perhaps, if you knew what I know. You would make an effort to get up and come along with me," said the guard.

"The right murderer will be in your place soon, and you will be out; so, collect your strength, my son, and go. I will help you. I have the strength to help you and I will do so."

"I hear someone talking, but I do not see anyone. Did you hear anyone?"

"Yes, I did. I heard the voice say, 'Son, get strength.' I heard that and more."

"'You will be out soon'—did you hear that?"

"I did."

Once more to "the carpet"—this time with more hope than before, that the truth would come out.

On entering I saw that the officer looked pale. He seemed to be very much worried.

"Good morning, sir. I have a very mysterious letter here. Can you tell me anything about it? You may read it."

I saw the words, "I am the real murderer of the mysterious woman ghost." I cried out:

"I prayed to God that the real murderer would come and acknowledge that he did the crime, for I knew that I did not, and I know who did."

"The name, sir?"

As he wrote it down, I could hear a hearty laugh, and so did he.

"Do not laugh, sir. You are not proved innocent."

"I beg your pardon. I did not laugh."

"Who did, then?"

"I am not able to say."

"Officer, take him back. I feel that I must see if this is a letter written by some crank, or was it written as a real confession. It is a mystery. I must say that I think this man is innocent, and I propose to look into this affair thoroughly at once. If he is innocent, he must be released. If not, he must work. I shall write to the authorities at the place where this letter was posted and have them make an investigation. I am of the opinion that this man is not guilty. As I sit here, I know that I am hearing the words: 'My son is innocent and you must release him from this prison.' Yet I know that the one whose voice I hear is invisible."

A week passed. There had been no answer from the ones who had been written to in regard to the prisoner. The superintendent grew weary of waiting. He felt that there should have been some reply. He had sent a copy of the anonymous letter of confession.

A guard appeared, and said: "You have a very sick man in 78. I have not been able to arouse him, and I have been working over him for some time."

Telling the story afterward, the superintendent said:

"I looked at the guard, and at that moment I saw a lady standing beside him. I arose and asked her: 'What can I do for you, madam?'

"The guard turned to look as she vanished, and said: 'You are mistaken. I brought no lady here with me.'

"I was so astonished at the remark that I spoke harshly and demanded the guard to tell me who the lady was and how she got in, if he had not admitted her.

"He replied: 'I am not able to say. I did not see anyone. I came directly to you and did not see anyone here, nor did I notice anyone near as I entered this office.'

"'Well, what is wrong, now?'

"'I came to tell you that No. 78 is a very sick man.'

"'I suppose he thinks that he will get his freedom after the reading of the mysterious letter, but I feel that there is a mystery in connection with the entire matter. There is not enough proof to entitle him to his freedom. Proof of that kind would not go in court—at least, not in this day and age. If he needs a doctor, call one.'

"'I am at a loss to know what to do with him.'

"As the guard turned to call a doctor for the prisoner, I heard a voice say:

"'He is not sick—only resting. He will soon be out of here.'

"I once more looked to see whence came the voice. But could gain no information as to where or from whom the voice came.

"'I must get away from this place. I am losing my mind,' I thought. 'Perhaps I really have lost it, for I can not explain these strange things. I must get away for a day or so. I will leave the office. Pearson can take care of this case while I am at rest and thinking this matter over. I can think it over away from here.'

"The guard returned in a few minutes, smiling, and with the news that the prisoner was sitting up when he arrived with the doctor. He also said that the prisoner had denied that anything was the matter with him.

"'So, he has been feigning, has he? Well, he shall get no more sympathy from this place. I have decided to rest a few days, and in my place, Mr. Pearson will give orders. But I want you to cease at once showing mercy on prisoner No. 78. You may go for Mr. Pearson. I shall leave directions for him to find a place for the prisoner and see that he works.'

"'I am not sure, but I think that I saw Mr. Pearson talking with the man very recently.'

"'Well, bring him here. I want to talk with him.'

"I was all a-tremble—just on the verge of nervous breakdown. All on account of this mysterious voice and seeing and not seeing.

"'Good morning, Mr. Pearson,' I said. 'I am leaving for a few days' rest, and I want you to take charge of this office and see that a convict here, No. 78, is put to work. He is very much averse to doing any work, and we have no pets in this place, so he can not be made one. The guard will report to you from time to time in regard to him.'

"As I was leaving, in an undertone I said: 'Yes, and if you do not get reports from some others, as well as the guard, I shall be very much disappointed. I hope that you will. I pray that you may, and perhaps I shall have help to find out what all this means. I hope that he will be able to explain all the mysterious actions by the time I return to work.'

"Oh, what a relief it was to know that I was away from that strain for a while, at least!"

The acting superintendent thought: "I am going to see what the trouble is with No. 78. I wonder if that is the fellow who has caused so many mysterious things to happen around here. By George! I believe it is. I will ask the guard. Here he comes."

"Guard, if that 78 prisoner hasn't any aptitude for the position he has to occupy, you may bring him in. I will try to find out what vocation he has followed, and see if we can accommodate him."

As the guard left, he shook his head, as if to say: "You can not have any luck in getting that fellow to work."

But the official in his own mind decided: "My dear old dad has often told me that kind words will do far more than harsh ones or harsh treatment. I am going to treat this prisoner with kindness and gentleness."

Then the acting superintendent looked up to see if he had a hard criminal to deal with, as No. 78 entered the door with his guard. He sank into his chair, gasping:

"What do I see? My brother! Do my very eyes deceive me, or is it really he? A convict in this place!"

CHAPTER VII

"My Brother a Convict!"

The official thought: "I must not let myself be known. I must not."

To the prisoner he said: "You may be seated, sir. I want to talk to you."

Then to the guard: "I will excuse you, guard. I wish to question the prisoner alone."

Turning to the prisoner: "Now, sir, I should like to hear something about yourself. Why were you sentenced, and have you registered under your real name?"

"I have, sir. I am not a criminal. I have been sentenced because of strong circumstantial evidence. I am innocent. I did not commit the crime for which I am here."

"Well, my opinion of you is good. I do not believe that you are a murderer—at least, I hope not. What occupation did you follow before you came here?"

"I was a follower of any work I could do—anything that my strength would permit me to do. I was not a disagreeable man. I made many friends."

"If you had many, your friends were no help to you in this case. Did not they offer any assistance?"

"No, sir; I was judged wrongly from the beginning—that is, as soon as it was discovered that it was my handkerchief which was found by the dead lady's side. My friends were nowhere to be found. I received cold and hard looks from all."

"Well, sir, I have heard your story. I want to ask you where you were born. What is your native country?"

"My home, sir, is in England. When a very small boy, I ran away from home. I have grieved my dear old mother so much. I understand that she has since died, and after I heard that, I never cared to go home again, but I feel that many times she has spoken to me. Often, when I have been attracted to company I did not know well, I could feel that she was near me and I could hear these words: '*My son, be careful, be careful!*' And I did not and would not go on after getting the warning, as I called it."

"You talk as if you had tried to live the right kind of a life, and I feel that you have, but in the position which I hold here I must not show any favors; otherwise I would do so in this case. Therefore, I must give you work to fit the crime of which you have been accused. That will mean hard work."

"I am willing to work, but do not give me work that my strength will not allow me to do. I am weak. I do not get the substantial food that you do, therefore I am not able to work hard. You do not know what it means to be punished for a crime committed by another. I am being punished for a murder which I never committed, and I ask you to have mercy on me."

"You are guilty until proved innocent. I will ring for the guard, and he will place you where you belong."

As the guard approached the prisoner turned and looked in astonishment. The official also looked, and, describing the scene afterward, he said:

"I was raised from my chair. I do not know by what means. Then I began to feel dizzy and could not speak. I lost my power to see. I could feel someone near, and then I heard the voice of a woman saying: 'You would sentence your brother to hard labor, to enable you to hold your own position? You, a child of the same mother and father? Have you no mercy on him? My son, take this brother to your arms and let yourself be known to him. Look into this affair and see if he is not innocent. I will release you, and you do with your brother as you would have him do to you. These are the commands of the spirit of your mother.'

"I shall never forget the terrible strain I was in, and as I mumbled brokenly, I felt a hand trembling, trying to help me to stand up, and I was given strength by the help of this hand.

"The guard asked for instructions as to where he should place this man—my brother, and I ordered him back to his cell.

"I was at a loss to know what to do. Must I confess—acknowledge him as my brother? or should I pretend to be ignorant of the fact which was plain to my mind? No one knew that he was my brother—not even the man himself knew it. Why should I acknowledge a criminal and a murderer? I could not!

"I thought: 'I shall place him at once at hard labor. I shall call the guard and have him brought in. I shall try to be brave and not think of boyhood days, when he and I went hand in hand to the dear old school. And dear mother, how she caressed us as she said good-bye! I can hear those words ring in my ears yet: "Run along, children, and study hard, and some day you will be your mother's pride." Yes, to-day, if she could be near her criminal son, she would not be so proud of him. She would do as I am going to do, disown him.'

"I had been so deeply engrossed in thought that I had not called for the prisoner, so I called: 'Guard, I want you to bring No. 78 in here.'

"I felt so uneasy that I thought: 'Can it be that I have decided wrong in this matter?'

"'Here he is,' responded the guard, in a short time.

"'Come in, and I will find the work for you to do which I think you will be able and trustworthy to do. You may take this coat and hat, and you may remove your coat of stripes, and we will exchange places.'

"'What! You think that I would not do my part if I were given work which I could do? I know that I would do my part if given work I could do. I know I would do my part. Oh, please give me a chance! I only want an opportunity to live, if I can, those ten years I must stay in here—or, at least, until I am proved innocent.'

"'Well, how do you think you can prove that you are innocent?'

"'The real murderer has written to the superintendent and confessed his guilt—or, at least, a letter has been sent here stating that I am innocent.'

"'You received such a statement?'

"'I did not, but the officer did—the one whose place you are filling.'

"'I will look into this matter, at once.'

"'You may take him back to his cell, guard, and I will send for him again when I have investigated this thoroughly. Take him back, and return at once.'

"I was sure that if he were innocent, he could be proved to be so, and I decided to go about it at once.

"'A great man, he is,' said the guard. 'We have had more trouble with him than with twenty-five of the other prisoners together.'

"'Do you know anything in regard to a letter written here?'

"'I do not. I think that the superintendent has taken a letter for use while he is working on the case for the poor devil.'

"'Well, I will go to the records and see if there is a record of any such letter.'

"'I hope that you will do something in a hurry, for I am getting tired of pacing back and forward with the gentleman,' said the guard. 'I feel that I have need of a pair of shoes sot to going some other direction than from 78's cell to the office and back.'

"'Well, Pat, what is your opinion of this case? Do you think the man is innocent, or not?'

"'I'm not here acting as judge, but if he is guilty, the mon should work. Setting around eating of the victuals and his time going on just the same!'

"'The only way to prove his innocence would be for the poor woman to come back and tell how the murder was done, and I don't think there would be any of us here to do time or see others did if we would see her here telling us how she was murdered.'

"'I, for one, would be a dead Pat.'

"'Well, Pat, we are both in doubt about the prisoner's guilt. Now, as long as he is here and proved guilty, say we find work for him to do. What would there be to do where a man could work and not work?'

"'Leave him have the same job he has had—rest in his cell when he is not on the road here and back.'

"'If you want a job of that kind, you misunderstand me, Pat. As I understand the poor man, he has never done very hard manual labor, and to place him to work of that kind, I fear, would make it necessary to soon change again. I am sorry that it had to fall to me to confine a convict to hard labor and feel that he is innocent [in an undertone] and my brother!'

"'Well, shall I bring the poor devil in? My shoes have pointed that way; every time I start the shoes on my very feet wants to track to 78's cell.'

"'I wish we could arrange everything, Pat, so your shoes could get a rest. It matters not about our minds. Bring him along.'"

CHAPTER VIII
The Brother Sentenced to Hard Labor

The official continued: "As the man left to do my bidding, I said to myself: 'He has gone to bring in my brother for me to sentence to hard labor. What shall I do? I do not feel as if I could utter the words.'

"I was completely upset. I experienced a most peculiar feeling. I thought: 'Here he comes. I must do my duty.'

"I said to the prisoner: 'Come in, sir. And how do your feel this morning?'

"Now, the devil take the mon who is two-faced! I brought the prisoner here to be put to work. Instead of that, he is having a nice visit with him. Inquiring about his health!' Pat was heard mumbling to himself.

"'Well, sir, I am going to see if you can do the work I will give you to do. I am going to have you take care of the prisoners in seeing that they have water to drink. Now, I will give you instructions. You understand the rules of the prison, and I hope that you will abide by them. Do not speak to any of your fellow-prisoners. You will be passing back and forth around each working booth. They understand how to ask for water, if they wish any.'

"'Pat, you may show him the way. And see that you do not burden him with a heavy load. Now you may go.'

"'Well, come along here, pet. I will give you a quart bucket which is light to carry, and if I happen to be going your way, I will help you carry it.'

"I hoped that at last we had found a place which the prisoner could fill. I felt somewhat at ease. I felt that I had done my duty to my brother as well as I could under the circumstances. I hoped that my arrangements would please him and also please the superior officer when he returned. And, by the way, it was time for him to return. I wondered if he had enjoyed his vacation.

"'Well, your honor.'

"'What is it, Pat?'

"'Your pet has refused to carry a full bucket of water, and stands there and looks at it as if he never saw water before. He will not speak a word. I do believe he is petrified—turned to one of those things which looks like a man and is a dead one.'

"'Pat, I can hardly believe you. I shall have to see for myself. Close the door behind us. We can not leave it unlocked to tempt our prisoners.

"'You are falsifying, Pat. Is not that the fellow, going there with that bucket of water?'

"'To be sure it is.'

"'Then why did you come to me with such reports?'

"'I came with the truth, your honor, and if the man can be dead one minute and alive the next, then I want to deal with the live ones all the time.'

"'You perhaps do not understand how to handle him.'

"'And faith, I think the majority of them is in the same fix. They have had the same experience themselves.'

"'Well, as long as everything is all right, we will try and rest easy.'

"'You are resting easy now. But when the superintendent comes back and finds that when he has left orders to punish a convict you favor him, I think you will have to find yourself another job.'

"When the superintendent entered, I experienced a feeling of relief. I exclaimed: 'Well, well! Back, and looking fine. I was thinking of you this morning, hoping that you were having a good rest.'

"'I did not rest much, for reasons that I will explain. I have here a letter, which I received before I left. It purports to have been written by the murderer for whom No. 78 is serving time.'

"'You have such a letter? But why do you look so excited?'

"'Have you had any trouble with the prisoner?'

"'Well, yes and no.'

"'What is the trouble? You answer me both ways.'

"'I have placed him to work, and after I had done so I was informed that he refused to work. I was anxious to see for myself, and when I went to investigate, I found him doing his duty. Therefore that is why I answered you as I did.'

"'To hard labor, as I instructed you to do?'

"'Well, yes, hard labor for him, as he explained that he had never done any hard labor. I hope that you will be pleased with the work I have given him to do.'

"'And what work has he been instructed to do?'

"'I have given—well, I thought he could be very useful in doing such work as that, and I asked Pat to start him at once.'

"'Yes, yes; I think that is a good job. Call Pat. Push button No. 9. Pat is an Irishman who will tell the truth.'

"'You are very nervous. I have noticed your peculiar actions ever since we began to talk of this affair.'

"'Good mornin', your honor. I am very glad to see that you have returned.'

"'I am glad to be here. Pat, what has become of No. 78? Is he working? I hope to have some knowledge of him when you have finished talking. I have not been able to find out much through Mr. Pearson, here.'

"Well, sir, I am only here to do as directed, and I follow instructions to the letter, and if I am told to go out and bate a fellow to death, I would do it, so in this case I did as I was instructed to do.'

"'You are a noble officer, sir. I think you have been requested to tell me what has become of No. 78. As yet you have not followed your instructions.'

"'I will bring the rascal in here and let him tell you what he is doing.'

"'Is he running at large, doing nothing?'

"'Yes, sir, and has the privilege of carrying some water along to take a drink when he gets thirsty.'

"'Bring him here. I will try to find out from him what orders have been given him.

"'I am going to see if I can solve this mystery. Mr. Pearson, are you ill? You are looking very pale. Do you feel ill? What is the matter? Are you faint?

"'Come along, Pat, step lively. Bring your prisoner in, and call Doctor Gray. Mr. Pearson is very ill.'

"The prisoner entered, saying: 'I am so glad to see you here and see you looking so refreshed.'

"'Yes, I think I shall hold my fresh looks a long time here and have a myth, like you, to deal with.'

"'I beg your pardon, sir, I have not caused you any trouble. I am not disobeying the rules. I never have.'

"'You are doing what now?'

"'I am carrying water for my fellow-prisoners to have a drink, as they need water so often.'

"'Come in, doctor. I have a patient here for you. Mr. Pearson is very ill.'

"At that moment I lost consciousness."

CHAPTER IX

The Superintendent Tries to Solve the Mystery

"Mr. Pearson has fainted. I have just returned from my vacation. Please get some water. I think it is nothing serious."

"I don't understand the case. His pulse is normal. His temperature is not high enough to indicate extreme illness. Yet he seems to be in a very deep faint. You had better call another doctor. I am at a loss to know what to do."

"I will ring for one at once. Here is Pat. I'll send him for Doctor Simson.

"Pat, go at once and bring Doctor Simson. We are not able to bring Mr. Pearson to."

Pat was heard mumbling to himself: "Another mysterious case. I'm going to leave this prison, and I would not blame the others if they did the same, prisoners and all."

"Dr. Simson, you are wanted at once, at the main office. The officer, Mr. Pearson, is a dead man—or, at least, he looks it."

"Well, Pat, if he is dead, there is no use in my going."

"You better go and see for yourself. There are some funny doings going on around here. Men look like dead ones, and not dead. I hope I won't be looking like a dead one and disappointing my friends. You must be coming along. They sent me for a doctor, and, faith, I would bring you at once."

"Well, Pat, I am ready. So, your patient looks like a dead one, hey?"

"You may decide that for yourself when you get there."

"Well, here we are. I shall soon see.

"Good morning, Mr. Officer. What have we here? A sick man?"

"Good morning, doctor."

"Doctor, what would you do in a case like this? I am not able to tell what is wrong."

"Have you taken his temperature?"

"I have."

"And what is it?"

"Normal."

"In so dead a faint, and normal?"

"You may take his temperature and see if I am mistaken."

"You are right, doctor. The best thing to do is to let the patient rest a few moments. I see no serious danger. I do not really understand the case."

"Pat, you may bring in the stretcher and we will take him to the hospital."

"I have been set to carrying the dead to the cemetery when they could not speak any more."

"You are having some trouble with one of your prisoners here, I understand."

"We are, doctor, and here he is."

"He does not look like a sickly man, but, my dear sir, you can not always tell by looking at a man what strength he has."

The prisoner interposed: "I am not a strong man, doctor, but I am strong enough to work if I were given work that I could do."

"We have placed him in many places, and we have not been able to find out what he can do."

"I am doing all that is required of me, am I not, at the last work you have given me to do?"

"You are, as far as I know, but you were sentenced here to hard labor. I must obey the orders of the courts."

"What is the poor man here for? He talks as if he were a good sort of a fellow."

"Murder. Does that sound as if he were a good fellow? And a poor woman, at that—strangled her to death. A horrible death."

At that moment a voice was heard saying: "You are accusing him wrongfully. He is not a murderer."

Turning to look for the speaker, they were surprised to see Mr. Pearson ready to speak.

"Well, sir, you have recovered. How do you feel?"

"I have not been ill."

"Well, we have been very busy for the last half-hour, trying to get you to speak."

"Pat, you may take the stretcher back. The patient will be able to walk to the hospital if he needs to go."

"The way these fellows have of dying and coming to life again must be a trade they have learned."

"Are you not going to let me work, sir, at what I was last given to do?"

"You are going to hard labor. No more of this playing off around here."

"Very well, sir."

"I don't think that you need my services any longer," said the doctor. "The officer seems all right, and he says that he is. I shall return to the hospital."

"Now, Mr. Pearson," said the superintendent, "please explain to me—when orders were given to put this man to hard work, you gave him a trusty job."

"I did the best I could. I am not a heartless man. The poor fellow said he could not do hard manual labor, and I believe he told the truth, and I am willing to give him a trial, for proof of his honesty."

"You know of all the crimes he has committed while in here, do you not? Or, at least, tried to and failed."

"In what way, pray tell me?"

"Trying to murder the guards. I, for one, had a peculiar experience with him. Found myself in the hospital—fortunately, not hurt, however, but not able to explain what had happened."

"Now you will have to work, sir, and I am going to call Pat. I can trust him to see that you do.

"Pat, take this fellow to the booth where they prepare iron for shipping, and see that he works. And I shall assign you, Pat, to take care of him, and him alone. We shall see if this mystery can be cleared up."

"Come along with me, pet 78. I will make a sure enough dead one out of you if you trifle with me. When I have instructions to do anything, I generally do it."

"Now, Mr. Pearson, I shall have to reprimand you. You are working under my instructions. I, bear in mind, hold a higher position over you, and you will have to explain to me the whys and wherefores of what you did, as you did not follow my directions."

"I followed your instructions, sir, the best I could, after Pat spoke of a letter which was received here by you, written as a confession of the crime for which this poor fellow was doing time."

"So, your sympathies got such a hold over you that you use the expression 'poor fellow,' do you? My opinion is that the letter was a hoax to get sympathy for him while here. It was probably written by some friend of the man's on the outside."

A voice said: *"You are accusing my son wrongfully, and you must suffer for it."*

"My God! Did you hear that?"

"Did I hear that? Yes, and I have heard that and more so many times that I have become quite familiar with the voice and do not feel alarmed at hearing it. Tell me what it was—*you!*"

"*You, you,* tell me what you think it was, and I will tell you something, then."

"Well, sir, I am not going to try to express myself, for I can not do so, but I will go back to my part of the work."

"You will remain here with me and express yourself as to what your belief is in regard to the mysterious voice we hear."

"Come, quick!"

It was Pat's voice.

"Come quick! The fellow is talking himself to death. I have bated him for half an hour and he is still talking, and devil a bit does he care for my bating."

"I will leave you and go with Pat."

"You will have to do something quick. He has disturbed the whole prison and the bating I gave him helped to excite the other prisoners' curiosity to know what the man was being beaten for."

"Right this way, I think, is the nearest, Pat. Avoid excitement as much as possible."

"You will see the poor devil throwing his hands and telling that he is not the murderer. And he is mumbling something about not going to be punished for a crime he never committed."

"You in trouble again? Not satisfied without disturbing the prisoners as well as the officials?"

"I beg your pardon, sir, I have been doing all I could do, and working, sir, since you placed me here. I felt a dizziness come over me. I don't know how long I stood before I regained myself."

"Do you feel as if you had had a good beating?"

"I? No, sir, I do not."

"Then the devil takes the man I will ever punish again," said Pat; "I've been working myself out of breath bating him and then he stands up there and tells that he didn't know he got a bating."

"You feel as if you could do the work, do you?"

"I will try, sir. It is awful hard and I feel I haven't strength to last the day through, but I will go as long as I can."

"Now, Pat, we will return to the office, and I want you to tell Mr. Pearson the trouble you had with this fellow, and while you are telling him, and telling how quietly he was working, you as well as I will watch Mr. Pearson's face and see how much sympathy, if any, goes out to the prisoner."

"Indeed, your honor, I have noticed the sympathy shown to the prisoner by Mr. Pearson, while you were away. He even offered to exchange coat and hat with the man, and job too."

"Pat, are you telling me the truth? A man holding the position which Mr. Pearson does, making such sacrifices as that with a prisoner, and one who is here sentenced for the crime which he is? Now, before we go in, I caution you to be watchful."

"Well, Mr. Pearson, a time we have had with the 78 convict, a murderer, and the worst hypocrite I ever saw."

"You found things as Pat represented them, did you?"

"No, I did not. The fellow was working very hard when we reached the place."

"The same thing occurred with me. I once hastened to investigate and found him as you did, doing his duty. So, sometimes, we are not to judge the poor prisoner too harshly, for we are not always informed correctly."

"I am here to speak for myself. I am the one who has informed you, as well you know, and I will prove to you, your honor," said Pat, "that I gave the man a good bating."

"Yes, that would not be hard for me to believe. You did that, but it would be hard to make me believe some of the reports that have been made against the prisoner."

"You seem to take a deep interest in No. 78. What is the secret, pray tell me?"

"I have no secret, sir."

"I have a secret which I shall tell some day, and you will believe me," *a voice was heard to say.*

CHAPTER X
Pat Allows the Prisoner to Escape

"I am going to leave you in charge of this place and I am going to investigate. I shall don a suit of one of the guards and follow this man around from morning until night and see if I will have any trouble with him.

"Come along, Pat. Find me a club. That is about the first thing I shall have to do—use it on goodness knows whom. But someone is going to get a punishment from me."

"If you find a job with the last fellow I had to bate, you will have a good job."

"Now, Pat, did you notice any strange actions about this mutt, Mr. Pearson? I did, and I am under the impression that some secret lies there, and the old saying is, 'Murder will out.'"

"You are not of the opinion that he is guilty of murder?"

"I see, Pat, that you do not understand me. I believe that Mr. Pearson knows this convict, in some way that he does not care to tell. There is a mystery there."

"Now, here is a club I have carried, and I know a good one. And if you want two, here is another."

"What would I do with two, Pat? One is all you can use at one time."

"Well, I'm thinking that if he had two clubs in his hands, as he was throwing them, I would never have been able to give him the bating I did."

"I hope that I shall not have to use one, Pat, much less two. Now, I am going to take charge of the prisoner, and, Pat, as I shall be close to him all of the time, you had better drop around to the office quite often and see how Mr. Pearson is getting along."

"I will do that, your honor."

"You may go—no, I will go alone, as I will then be less liable to be noticed."

"Very well. Good luck to you and your new job."

"Now for the mystery to be solved," said the superintendent. "I shall follow that fellow until I satisfy myself who is right and who is wrong. And I shall find out if Pat is as faithful as he has been supposed to be. I feel that the accused man has someone to help him in all of this work, but who the helper is, that I should like to know."

As he approached the prisoner the superintendent said: "I thought that I would take care of you for a while—or, at least, try to. I see that you are doing very nicely, and I am glad. I hope that you will try and live up to the rules. You may speak to me when spoken to, but do not speak without being spoken to."

"I am going to pass by and take a peep at our new officer, and see how he likes his job," said Pat. "Well, he jabbers, he is not here!

Where in the deuce has he gone? Say, do you hear me? Shake this door if you do. Shake, and if you don't speak, shake anyway.

"Well, I'll have to find out if he drew his wages and quit his job, without giving the firm notice. Hello! hello! Well, the only thing I can do is to go for the other fellow. I think he has got a key. Perhaps the next fellow that gets the job will be me.

"What in the deuce do I see, away back in the corner? As sure as I am alive, it is him. Well, well, wake up! You have got an easy job, I know, but I don't think you need to lay down and go to sleep by the side of it.

"Well, I can't wake the poor devil, but I know someone who can. And I would hate to be in the poor devil's shoes if that one comes in and finds him slapin'. So, here's to the office and report, as I promised to do, if I lose my job by doing so. Someone is sure going to lose his job here, and that very shortly."

"Well, Pat, what are you doing around here?" said the superintendent. "Why are you looking so excited? I am getting along fine here."

"Well, I am not getting along fine there."

"What is wrong, Pat?"

"The fellow that you left in your office has laid down and gone to sleep on the job. And he locked the door before he did so. He was very careful that no one could get in or out."

"Gone to sleep? And the door locked? Here, you watch this man and I will see what is the meaning of this."

"If he doesn't get his nap out before the officer gets there, it will be a pity."

"Here! What is wrong, Mr. Pearson?"

"Wrong? Nothing is wrong."

"Where have you been?"

"I have been here, sir, and very busy."

"Now, Mr. Pearson, were you not asleep with the door locked on the inside?"

"I am not guilty. Pat has been giving you some more reports—and false ones, if he has told you that I was sleeping. I have not felt well, in the last thirty minutes. I felt a dizziness come over me, but I feel all right now."

"Do you know if you were asleep at any time, or in a faint, while you were feeling dizzy?"

"I was not, sir. I was sitting at this desk, as you see me."

"And I am being deceived by one in whom I have placed confidence. Pat is a good fellow. I can not believe that he would deceive me. Perhaps, after all, I had better watch him, as well as the other one," thought the superintendent. "I need help. I have too many to watch. I can not be here and there too, but I will stay by the prisoner until I have satisfied myself that he is right or wrong."

"Come quick! Help! help! The fellow has turned into a woman and it looks as if there were half a dozen people where he is," called Pat; "and he speaks like a woman. All he would have to do would be to put on a woman's clothes and you would let him pass out on her voice, be jabbers! She might be cultivating the voice to make her get away, but when they get by Pat they will have to go when I am asleep, for I am not here to let anyone get away without their papers of freedom. You will have to come, as the prisoners are killing time, listening to the lady speaking."

"Now, office superior," said Mr. Pearson, "you have so much confidence in Pat, leave him in charge of the office, and I will go with you to see what is wrong with the prisoner—78."

"I will do that."

"Pat, take care of this office until we return. Come along, Pearson. Make haste, this way."

"Well, I felt all along I would be the man to fill this place, and some day this Irishman will be called the 'superior officer' around this prison. I hope they will succeed in finding the lady still talking—or the gentleman, whichever it is."

"Well, officer, do you see anything wrong? The fellow is working."

"I do not understand this, and no excitement among the prisoners."

"Well, I say the trouble is in the false reports made by Pat."

"We will go back to the office and I shall ask Pat to explain what he meant by causing all this excitement by false reports. Now that we are on the way back to the office, I want to talk to you about those mysterious voices. How do you account for them? Well, I was in hopes you would be able to tell me something. What have you heard, Pearson?"

"I have heard more than I care to hear again."

"You are not frightened, are you?"

"Well, I am not praying to hear any more of it."

"I am going to say to Pat that he is not fooling anyone any more; the next time he comes with such stories, he will be sent back to take care of his own trouble. What, the office door open? What does that mean? Where is Pat?"

CHAPTER XI
The Mystery Deepens

"I think Pat has left the place. After all his false reports, he will, or perhaps has, felt that he will be discharged, and will go before notice is given."

"Here he comes. Well, Pat, what do you mean? Is that the way you do when trusted with the care of this office? Did I not say to you that I had all confidence in you? And now you have given me cause to doubt you in all things."

"Your honor, would you have confidence in me at all if I would sit here and let the prisoners all walk out? Just about two minutes ago a lady came to the office and asked to come in. After I opened the door, she just walked right through the office and out of the door. I called to her to halt, and she did not stop, and I made a start for her, and in all my life I never saw a female get the space between her and me as she did."

"Do you mean to tell me that you have let some of the prisoners get away?"

"I mane to tell you that the lady that came through that door got away—prisoner, or whatever you may call her."

"Pat, I am not going to discharge you now, for I shall have to see what convict it was and what was her sentence here. Then I shall be better able to deal with you. I am sorry, Pat, that you have proved to be such an untrustworthy guard, and I, as well as Mr. Pearson, here, have found you to be misrepresenting things all along and causing any amount of trouble. Now you may go and do what the last orders gave you to do, and I will take care of my man. If you find any stranger things around here, don't come to me. I shall not go to investigate another call from you. Now go."

"Your honor, I would like to speak a word in my own behalf. I am not as you have expressed yourself that I was, untrustworthy. I will swear to my Father in Heaven that I have been honest, honest in all my actions, and when I called for help, you were informed right. I gave the correct reports, and I want to say now that if you have that kind of opinion of me, I will lave the prisoners and you may look for another Pat. I am not a thief. If so, I would be wearing the stripes instead of the blue, and I feel I have been misjudged. I hope that you will find out that Pat was just what you thought, true and trustworthy, and I will say to you that you had better keep an eye on your fellow-officer, Mr. Pearson. I feel that he has caused you to form the opinion you have."

"Pat, go and do your duty, and all will work out right by and by."

"I will, your honor; but whenever you want the club I carry, the same is yours for the asking. I am ready to quit when I am not the gentleman I should be."

"Pearson, have you ever had any trouble with Pat?"

"I have not."

"I believe that you and he have not the best of feeling for each other. Can you explain the condition?"

"I have no grievance against Pat. I do not understand why he should bring in such alarming reports, reports which on investigation prove to be untrue, absolutely untrue, with no base or foundation whatever, and that is why I am not particularly fond of Pat."

"It is all a very strange affair. During my absence did you have a conversation with Convict 78? And what was the object of that conversation? What was your reason for dismissing Pat, after he had brought the convict in?"

"I do not remember doing so."

"I have been informed that you did. There should be no secrets among the officials and the prisoners."

"I am going to explain. I am the mother of these two boys, and the Prisoner 78 and my son Pearson, here, are brothers. Pearson knows that his brother is an innocent man, but is ashamed to acknowledge his brother. But the prisoner is as innocent as you, who are trying to punish him for a crime he never committed."

"Do you hear that voice, Pearson?"

"I do, but from whom does it come? There is no one here that I can see."

"*You will see me*," the voice was heard to say.

"'I will see you.' Did I hear that? Did you get that, officer?"

"I did, and I heard more; I heard the same voice say that you and this man, Convict 78, were brothers. Did you hear that?"

"I did."

"Well—"

"I am not sure of it. I only know that he carries my name, and his Christian name is the same as that of a brother of mine whom I have not heard from in years. He ran away from home when a small boy, and we never heard from him afterward. We thought he was dead, as he never returned or wrote. Poor mother grieved herself to her grave for that lost, wayward son. I remained home with her until she died."

"And the estate—did you advertise for him?"

"My father died when I was a small boy and left mother in good circumstances. I and this brother who left home were the only heirs."

"And you got the bulk of the estate? Did I understand you to say that you advertised for your brother?"

"Well, you see, it was this way: not hearing from him for so many years, I decided that he was dead, and I did not think it worth while."

"You are not sure that this is not your brother, then, Mr. Pearson?"

"No, I am not sure."

"Well, I will send for him and we perhaps may be able to find out by questioning him. Ring for Pat."

Just then Pat, mumbling, "I will stroll around and see if the superior officer has changed his mind about me being a gentleman," appeared.

"Here is Pat, now."

"Pat, bring in No. 78, at once."

"Whenever the man says 'Pat,' I know that 78 is wanted. Well, if that don't bate anything! I wonder now what he has done? I know that he has been good the last half-hour, for I have been watching him with my own very eyes, and devil take the one that has lied on him, now. Look at the poor fellow! He has the same feeling that I have. Every time he sees me coming, he knows that he is wanted.

"Well, you are wanted at the office, and come along quick, and have it over with. I feel very queer—I feel like I have eaten a fly for my breakfast. Only a different feeling comes on a fellow so quick when something is going to happen, and you don't know what it is.

"Your honor, do you want him now? If so, here he is."

"If I did not want him, Pat, I should not have sent for him. You may be seated over there."

"You see, the convict is sometimes treated with poor courtesy. Then I—I have not been asked to have a chair," Pat was mumbling to himself.

The officer turned to the prisoner:

"You are enrolled here in the name by which you were christened, are you not?"

"I am, sir."

"Clarence Pearson, is that your real name?"

"It is, sir."

"Do you remember anything about your people?"

"I do, sir."

"Tell me all you know about your family, and the number of children, brothers and sisters, and if your parents are living, and where you were born."

"I was a small boy when I left home, many years ago. My father I don't remember much about. My poor dear mother has often told me that I was quite young at the time of his death. I have no sisters. I have one brother, who was at home when I left. I have since heard that my dear mother has died. After I heard that, I never had the heart nor courage to go home again."

"Was your mother in comfortable circumstances?"

"Oh, yes, sir! My mother was a wealthy woman."

"And you will swear that that is your name?"

"I will, sir."

"Pat, you may take him back."

"You will not close the iron doors behind my child again! He is far more a free man, or should be, than the one sitting there in silence."

"Well, Pat, why don't you take him? He is ready."

"So, am I, but when you tell me to do a thing, and then tell me not to, how in the name of common sense do I know what to do?"

"I have given you only one instruction, and that was to go."

"Well, then, who the devil told me not to take him?"

"Did you get such orders?"

"I did."

"When?"

"Just now, and I got more than that."

"What did you get?"

"I heard a voice—where it came from, I don't see, but my hearing is good—and this is what it said—I will look about me and see that I am not knocked down after I tell what I heard."

"Go on, and tell what you heard."

"Faith, and I will tell every word of it. I heard—as you finished telling me to take him back—I heard a voice say: 'The doors will not close behind—'"

"I can't think what is the matter, Pat."

"I am getting them. I will be a dead man, here, soon, like some of the other ones around here has been. Anyway, I didn't take the man back, did I?"

"Pat, you are acting funny. What is the matter with you?"

"Come along here! I will lock *you* up if you are the guilty one."

"Pat, you are not going to take Mr. Pearson. He has not committed a crime."

"I say, come along here! You are the thief, to rob your brother of all and then sit and let him suffer."

"You are going mad, Pat. I shall have to call for help if you do not turn Officer Pearson loose."

"Call for help. All the power you have in this prison could not conquer me."

"I shall turn in a general alarm if you do not let him go."

"Turn in your alarm. I am ready to fight for my innocent son's freedom, and you too know that he is not a murderer, yet you sit there and allow him to suffer, and for another's crime. Here is the murdered woman standing here declaring his innocence—and the real murderer is her husband, and you have not made an effort to find him. Go look for him. Place my innocent boy in a closed room, if you like, but never behind bars. I will free him, as I have done all the time here, if you dare to place him behind bars again!"

"You will fall, Pat. Sit down. Here, steady, now. Give me some water quick. Have some water, Pat. He looks so queer. Oh! you feel all right, Pat?"

"I am not ailing. Why do you ask me if I feel all right? The only thing I see, I was standing up a while ago, and now I am sitting down."

"Yes, Pat; you were acting very funny, and insisted on taking Officer Pearson to jail, instead of No. 78."

"Faith, I think he will be there soon enough."

"I don't understand you. I am going to make you suffer for that talk. I shall not allow myself to be called a thief by my inferiors. I shall have a settlement with you, sir. Either you or I will leave here, and I think that you will be the one to go."

"Don't be too sure of that. You may be wearing stripes around here yourself, and I, the common Irishman, telling you what to do and throwing the bread and water at you."

"Hey, Pat! What do you mean? Why are you doing all this talking? Are you accountable for what you are saying? I shall have to stop this talk at once. We are not in the habit of allowing our employees to talk in that manner."

"I think that Pat has served his time here. He is beginning to think that he is the boss."

"Well, I'd like to say the same thing about you in regard to serving time, but I don't think you have started in on your time yet, and when your brother who is sitting here tells all he knows, you will be wearing his clothes and he will be wearing something better, for some of that money belonging to him which you have will enable him to do unto you as you should do unto him—and that is, help when in trouble."

"Pat, I am speaking to you for the last time, and I shall have to discharge you if you do not quiet yourself."

"You will not discharge him."

"Well, did you decide what to do? Shall I take 78 back?"

"Pat, you talk and look and act quite differently now. What was wrong? Do tell."

"I am just the same Irishman. Do you think I have changed in looks? I hope not, for who ever saw a homely Irishman?"

"You did change in looks, but look all right now. Put the prisoner in the other office—No. 2. I may need him soon. Then you may go."

"Well, Mr. Pearson, what does all this mean? I don't understand. But I shall not cease the investigation until I find out what is wrong."

"You are paying too much attention to what Pat has been saying."

"I am not referring to Pat's sayings. I am asking you, or will do so, to explain about this man bearing the same name and having the same birth-place and the same number in his family as you have told me that you have. Your statements were identical, and do you not know that this is your brother? I believe that he is, and why do you not want to acknowledge him, or find out whether he is guilty or innocent?"

"How often, sir, do we meet men who have the same name as ourselves—many times the surname and the Christian name are the same. I am under the impression that this is one of those times."

"And I am very sorry, Pearson, but I am thinking that, although it is very unfortunate for you, this is not an accident."

"I do not understand you, sir."

"Well, then, I will make it plainer. I think that the convict here is your brother, and you know it."

"You are judging me too harshly. I am not deserving of that opinion from you."

"You must do something to prove your innocence; otherwise I shall notify the authorities and lay the circumstances before them."

Pearson was silent.

"You have my sympathy, but we should show no partiality in our dealings with our fellow-men. They must be treated fairly. Even prisoners must receive justice. I shall leave you to think this matter over, and you may report to me, later, how you feel about the matter."

"I have nothing to think over and decide on."

"Then you will acknowledge that you are his brother?"

"I may be, and if I am, I shall only be by birth. I shall never claim a murderer for a brother."

"You are accusing him wrongfully. He is not a murderer."

"Pearson, for God's sake, where did that voice come from?"

"I can not tell."

"Then I will show myself."

"Mother, mother, mother! Help! help!"

"Well, I have stayed away long enough. I think it's about time they were doing something to the poor convict." It was Pat's voice, this time. "Perhaps I will be needed. I hear a call for help. I may find the whole bunch dead."

"Come quick, Pat!"

"What in the — is the matter, now?"

"I was talking to Pearson, and he threw up his hands and cried out, 'Mother!' three times, and called for help. He has fainted. You had better call a doctor, or go for one; the wires may be busy."

"Yes, I think the wires is crossed at this end, and I am believing someone will lose his job before they get them straightened, and if it is me, I am willing to go. Many a poor devil would be glad to lose his job here. I hope I find the doctor in and not busy. The poor officer may get tired laying in a fit so long."

"Well, Pat, you have got another dead man for me to take care of, have you?"

"That is what I came for, and you had better make it lively. The superior officer doesn't feel very comfortable over the affair."

"You mean that I am wanted at the office?"

"And I would not be saying so if you were not wanted."

"Well, Pat, I sometimes think that you are like the Dutchman. I must take you as you mean, and not as you say."

"You had better get a move on you, for I mane it."

"You are walking so fast I can not keep up."

"Indeed, he told me to go for you because I go faster than the wires, and I want to keep up my reputation with the boss."

"You are trying to make a record for yourself, are you?"

CHAPTER XII
Another Dead Man

As the two entered the office the superintendent exclaimed: "You are slow about getting here. I believe Mr. Pearson is dead."

"I hope not," replied the doctor; "but I will see in a moment." Then: "Pulsation very weak. Did he complain of feeling ill before he collapsed?"

"No, doctor; only some excitement and—"

"He seems to have been affected very deeply from it. I am alarmed."

"Do you think that we should send for more help?"

"I am not of the opinion that they could do any more than I am doing."

"You are going to need the stretcher."

"To the 78 cell, doctor! And a stretcher to carry out the dead live ones!"

"Pat, step inside and see what is the matter with No. 78. I hear a noise."

"I am going to have the club ready. I am not feeling very good, and I don't think it would take much to get me—bated."

"Now, doctor, I have a secret to tell you. I have been mistrusting a convict's relationship to an employee of this office, and I have asked him for a complete explanation of the affair. I understand that he has shown some favors to the convict in my absence. And I can not, for the life of me, explain what the voices are that we hear in this office, at times, pertaining to this officer. He and I were here talking the matter over, and I asked him if he did not know this man was his brother. He said that he did not. At that moment we heard a voice, '*I will show you!*' and a terrible scream came from him, and as he looked up, he called his mother three times for help, and fell as you see him."

"I have witnessed many fainting spells, but never did I find the pulse in such a condition."

"Officer," came the voice of Pat, "I am having a picnic, hearing the prisoner talk in his sleep, and with his eyes open. Would you mind coming in and getting some of the news?"

"You may go," said the doctor; "I will take care of the patient. There is nothing that you can do."

"Very well, I will see what is wrong.

"Well, Pat, you seem to be having a free entertainment."

"You will have to name it. I call it a treat to see a fellow talk asleep and standing, with his eyes open all the time he is sleeping."

"What is he talking about?"

"Listen, for yourself. He is going on so fast I can't run and keep up."

"I am telling you I am innocent. I did not murder, and I am not guilty, and my brother who was in a faint is all right now, and I am the spirit of the mother of those two boys—my sons, and I have been the mysterious one whose voice you have heard here trying to tell you and help my son out of this trouble. I have to explain this by inspiring my son, as I am doing now, and I can do so, as you see. And I have brought the woman who was murdered with me, and she is here to say that she was strangled to death by her husband, not by my son. My son is not guilty of that crime, and I want you to take this name and address which she will give me, and send for the real murderer. His name is Robert Devenart, and Mrs. Devenart is here to tell you all about the crime, and I will repeat the words after her:

" 'I was strangled to death, not by this man here, but by my husband. I will tell all. I was having trouble with him and as he threatened me, I screamed, and the door opened, and this man, whom I knew slightly, entered and asked if he could be of any assistance. I tried to be brave, and told him that I did not need any assistance. He left, with an apology for intruding. Then my husband clutched me by the throat and choked me to death. Turn this man out and bring the real murderer in. Your officer is all right. I will go now.' "

"Very well, doctor."

"Do you feel all right, Pearson?"

"I am all right. I'll just step out for some fresh air."

"I am not satisfied to think that he was in a faint, officer. I have never come in contact with anything like it in my whole experience as a physician. You had hardly left the room until he opened his eyes and looked around."

"Had it not been for the fact that I might have missed some of the words that were being spoken, I should have called you, doctor. I stepped into the room, and there he—the prisoner, I mean—was standing, talking, his eyes open and apparently, he was himself. I inquired of Pat what was wrong, and he—the prisoner—answered by saying, 'I am not guilty.' The murderer's name was given, and many more things were said, which I dare not mention now."

"Here is Pat."

"Well, give me my time. I am a brave Irishman, I can bate a fellow to death if need be, but I am not brave enough, when the dead come around and talk to me, to stick around any longer. Faith, I did not see anything, but I surely heard, and I know that I will fall dead if I ever see one of the dead ones walking around here."

"Pat, I can not give you your time. You are needed here. Go along and do your duty, and I will send for you if you are wanted."

"I hope you will never send for me if the dead want me."

"Pat is a good, trusty fellow, and, doctor, I am glad I can make a confidant of you in this matter. I am given the address of a person. I am going to write at once to the proper authorities and see if they can find the name, a very strange name. I never heard it before. I don't think they can get the wrong fellow if they find one by that name."

"I would advise you to investigate, officer. People are oftentimes innocent, although apparently proved guilty by law, and I am prejudiced against circumstantial evidence. Many poor men are serving time because of that kind of evidence."

"I am going to thank you—"

"Did you speak? Did you?"

"No, doctor. You have heard some of that voice which we hear so often. Can you explain?"

"No, sir; and I do not intend to stay in here to hear any more of it, or to try to explain it. Good-bye."

"Good-bye, doctor."

"I am going to ask you to allow me a vacation, officer. I am not feeling very well."

"Mr. Pearson, I have some very important work to do in the next few days, and I shall need you badly."

"I should like to leave by the first of the week, if possible."

"It is more than likely that you can do so. You have nothing more to say in regard to the affair of which we were talking?"

"I have not. I do not feel that this man is any relation to me, therefore I am not going to bother anything about him."

"What was your birth-place, Pearson?"

"I have secrets of my own. I don't think that you or anyone should ask about them, and I refuse to tell you. I am not being tried for any crime. I do not have to answer your questions."

"Very well. You may go back to your old position. I shall look after the office. Say, Pearson! Here! You may take along the prisoner here. I don't care to have him in this room, keeping me alert at every noise."

To the prisoner Pearson said: "Come. I will put you in your cell."

"I am willing to go—to do anything that you request me to do."

"Clarence—did I understand you to say that was your name?"

"Yes, sir."

"Here is your cell. Step in. I will also go in. I want to talk to you. Clarence, do you remember anything about your old home, and your brothers and sisters, and your father and mother?"

"I have no father—he died when I was a small boy, and sisters I have none. I have one brother."

"What was your father's name? Of course, I know it was Pearson, but what was his Christian name—or have you forgotten it?"

"I have not forgotten anything about my home. I remember all very well. It seems only yesterday; I have such a vivid recollection of all. My brother's name was William O. Pearson."

"What was the *O.* for?"

"For Oliver, and I often called him by that name. You have such a strange way of looking at me, officer. Do you not believe me?"

"Yes, Clarence, I believe you. I am going to tell you why I look at you so strangely. You are my brother, and I am going to make this right with you, if you will change your story and say that you changed your name when you got into this trouble—or, rather, that you have gone under an assumed name since you committed this crime. If you will do as I say, at the end of your term, I will give you five thousand dollars—when you walk out of this place a free man."

CHAPTER XIII
An Attempt to Bribe the Prisoner

"I have been a wanderer, and have eaten many a back-door hand-out, but I have never stolen nor murdered. I did not commit this crime. You, my brother, are free, and have money to bribe me with, and yet you do not care enough for your own flesh and blood to look up the real murderer. I do not want your money. I have two strong arms, and can work, as I have always done."

"Then you would work all your life, a poor man, rather than accept a little bribe, would you?"

"Yes, under the circumstances, I would. I feel that in the end I will be better prepared to meet my dear mother, when called home, than you will be. Did I not have something coming to me from the estate? My mother was a wealthy woman when I left home."

"Well, we had many reverses in business affairs, and she died practically a poor woman."

"I may be spared to live my sentence here if I am not found innocent and discharged, and then I shall return to the old home and investigate affairs and see if I am not entitled to a share in my dear mother's estate."

"Why can you not believe me? I have explained. She died practically a poor woman."

"You are not a poor man, are you, brother?"

"Well, I have a comfortable home."

"Is that all you have?"

"I do not feel disposed to explain everything to you."

"Where were you to get the five thousand dollars to bribe me with? Have you got that much money besides your comfortable home?"

"I shall have ten years to get that."

"Oh! you are buying me to commit a crime and have no money to give me after I have done so?"

"As I have stated, you are here for ten years. At the time of the expiration of your term I would in all probability have that amount."

"May I ask you why you wish me to deny my name?"

"Well, Clarence, I am holding a good position here, and I could not, perhaps, if it were known that I had a brother inside of these walls. Besides, I have a family in society, and it would injure them if this should all come out."

"You are thinking of yourself and your family and society, and not once have you given your poor brother a thought of sympathy. And he is innocent of crime."

"I am trying to help you. Have I not offered you five thousand dollars at the end of your term?"

"You are not helping me. No, sir. I have registered under my own name, given me by my dear parents, and I have no cause to disown it. I did nothing to disgrace it, and I am not going to be tempted with your money."

"I am sure that you will regret this, Clarence. I would favor you in many ways while you were serving your sentence."

"Could you not do so, as you are one of the officials, without my doing as you wish me to do?"

"Well, no. I should be suspected."

"Then how could you do so if I did as you request me to do—disown my name?"

"Well, well!"

"You are doing wrong, Oliver, to try to get me in deeper instead of helping me out. Why don't you go out and look up the real murderer and prove your brother innocent? I am quite sure I should not disgrace you if it were proved that I had been sent here an innocent man."

"You see, after one has been behind prison bars, he is always looked down upon by the public."

"But not in the eyes of God. He knows the guilty from the innocent."

"Then you feel that you would rather stay in prison and work ten years, and go out a broken man and penniless, than to receive five thousand dollars, as I have promised you?"

"If I have to lie for it, I'll take the poverty and peace of mind."

"I am sorry for you, Clarence, and I shall return and have another talk with you some day. Perhaps you will change your mind. Good-bye."

"I thank you, brother, for the word spoken just now. Yes, my brother, you have a comfortable home and a family in society, and an innocent brother in prison for ten years."

"You have the habit of talking to yourself, have you?" It was Pat who spoke.

"It helps a fellow, Pat, sometimes, when alone, to talk to himself."

"I am sure I heard two voices in here. I was after looking for a convict who occupied the next cell, 79, and I felt rather uneasy about you, and I thought I would see what you were doing, and I heard a very strange conversation in here."

"Pat, did you hear all that was said?"

"Sure, I did. What was I listening for if not to hear what was said?"

"And did you see anyone leave here?"

"Sure, I did. When I see a man passing this way, I looked to find if he was a broke-away."

"And will you—"

"I will keep my mouth shut until I have to open it."

"And would you tell all you heard?"

"Indeed, I would. Well, I think I will be going along. I will stroll by the office and see if he looks any the better off since he could not get rid of his five thousand dollars."

"Pat, you always come just in time. Take this letter to the office. I want it to go out on the first mail. If I wait for it to be taken up, it would not get off on the first mail. Make haste, as I am quite anxious for this to go."

"You can depend on it going if I have to take the train and carry it myself."

To himself: "Well, I wonder what the rush was. I will pick up the torn pieces when I get the chance, and see what this means."

"Mr. Pearson," said the superintendent, "I am called to attend to some business affairs. I shall leave you in charge of the office. I may not return until late."

"Very well, sir."

"Well, I just made the train. The next time I would like a few minutes to think between this place and the train. I never went so fast in all my life. I would be a good messenger. I could get the bad news to them in a hurry, as all of the confounded things have bad news in them.

"There comes Pat. I will give him the order I left with Pearson.

"Pat, I am going on some business, and I want you to put all of those torn pieces of paper in the fire and burn them up. I do not want anyone to see them. I made some errors and re-wrote the letter," said the superintendent.

"Now you have gone," said Pearson, "I will take care of those torn pieces of paper. Here is an envelope addressed to the place where Clarence committed the murder, and here is all of the letter. Now I'll see what was the cause for rush."

The letter ran as follows:

"I am writing you for help in looking up the case of a convict by the name of Clarence Pearson. I have every reason to believe that he is innocent of the crime for which he is serving sentence. Wire me if you have a name in the directory of your city like this: Devenart. If there is such a man, hold him for murder."

"My God!" gasped Pearson. "What does this mean? I am lost. I feel that they will find him innocent, and I guilty of crime; and I have sworn to the death of Clarence, so that I might receive his share of the estate. Now it is all to come out."

"Well," said Pat, "I met the officer, and he told me to clean up around and destroy the papers he has written on, and I don't see any."

"I had nothing to do and I put things in order," said Pearson.

"Where did you throw the scraps?"

"I put them in the fire."

"Did you lave the office to do it?"

"No, I did not leave the office."

"Then where is the fire you put them in? I was told to burn them and I must obey orders. If you did not burn them, I will be after doing it."

"You are always meddling in someone's affairs, Pat. You go along. I am taking care of this place."

"And I'm thinking you are taking care of some things in this place—at least, I would like to see those torn pieces of paper."

"You may go to No. 78's cell and see if he wants to come here. I would like to talk with him. Perhaps I can get some idea of the kind of work he could do."

"I will obey you. Now it is up to the poor convict to take his choice of work. And if he pleases to come, he can."

To the prisoner: "Well, are you asleep? Would you like to take a walk over to the office? Now, you don't have to go if you don't want to."

"I am willing, Pat, to do anything I am asked to do."

"You are very obliging. I'm sure I would be pleased if all the convicts would be as agreeable as you."

"You may bring him in, Pat, and then go to your work. I shall not need you any more at present," said Pearson.

"I'll go, but devil a bit will I work. I don't think anyone needs me now, and I'll just sit down here until someone does need me."

"Clarence, you have been thinking this over, have you—what we were talking about? I hope you will be sensible now, and make up your mind to do as I want you to."

"You want me to swear that I am not Clarence Pearson?"

"Yes. You will be helping yourself by so doing."

"Well, then, I will."

"That will help you to look forward for something to live on ten years from now."

"Well, what can I do to help you out of your trouble?"

"My trouble? I am not in trouble."

"You are not worried over my not doing as you requested me to do?"

"No. Only for your own good."

"Then tell me, if I change my mind when the time comes to deny it, what harm could it do you?"

"I should have to—"

"Finish what you were going to say."

"I'll tell you all, Clarence, if you will promise me that you will do as I want you to."

"Well, tell me, brother."

"I am going to make a clean breast of it all."

"I think I had better be getting up closer," whispered Pat. "I may think I'm hearing and not hear, for I am looking for the poor devil to tie a noose around his neck before he gets through with the clean breast he spoke of."

"Go on, Oliver; tell me. You are talking to your brother. You need not fear my betraying you—never, Oliver!"

"You left home, Clarence, when a small boy. You never wrote and poor mother and I mourned you as dead. Years afterward mother died, and, not knowing where you were, I was called upon to swear that you were dead, and I did so. In that way I fell heir to all of the estate, which was numbered in the hundred thousands. And, not knowing of your whereabouts, I decided to invest it, and I lost it all, except what I have told you of."

"I do not see the point in your demanding that I deny my name."

"Do you not see that I have sworn falsely to obtain the money, and you know that places me just where you are to-day, Clarence."

"Only you are guilty, Oliver, and I am not."

"I believe I'd better not listen any more. I am knowing too much. I may not be able to hold any more in me head, for I have it crammed full now, and I have got to keep it there till I can let it out, a little at a time, and it takes a man a long time to tell the judge and keep from telling what he don't want to."

"I know that I am guilty, but you can save me if you will."

"Brother Oliver, I am sorry for you and I will do all I can for you. I will do as you have asked me to do."

"Thanks, dear brother. And I shall be a brother to you while you are in prison."

"Now I think they have all the secrets told, and I'll walk around and see if I can persuade the officer to tell me where the fire was. He was so obliging to do my work for me," mumbled Pat.

"Come along, Pat; you may take the fellow back," called Mr. Pearson.

Pat to himself: "Oh! he is being called a 'fellow,' is he? If I bring him here to the office many more times, he will be a gentleman, not a convict."

Aloud: "Come along here! Back to your resting-place. Indeed, that is all you have done lately—rest."

The acting superintendent mused: "Now that Clarence is going to deny his name, I can see my way out of this. I shall not take my vacation now. I must stay and see this thing through. So, my superior officer has written to where the murder was committed and asked for a wire in answer. And we may look for one to-morrow, as the letter went out on the early train. It will be received in the morning, and a wire will be received some time in the evening."

"Well, 'fellow,' here is your place to rest till I come for you, and you may look for me soon, at that," remarked Pat as he placed the prisoner in his cell.

CHAPTER XIV
The Convict's Prayer

As the superintendent entered the office on his return he said to Pearson: "I am back. I have been looking up some of your history in the past."

"I do not understand you, officer."

"You will, however."

"Why are you looking up my reputation?"

"I have every cause to do so. I see that you have the same name as the convict, or he has the same name as you have. Of course, that is nothing unusual, for two men often have the same family name, and even Christian name; but you are favoring this prisoner in many ways, which looks suspicious. I have never noticed that you favored other prisoners, and I do not believe that you would do so without some secret reason, in this case."

"I have only tried to treat him humanely."

"I see the humane part of it, Pearson."

"I think I will walk around and see how the fellow is looking after he has spent this five-thousand-dollar bribe and got the poor convict to deny his own name. I wonder what he will take for a name if he denies the one, he has got. For the love of Mike, I hope it won't be Pat! Indeed, I don't want to have a name like any one of the prisoners in here, and, thank God! the place has no Pats. An Irishman is too slick to come here against his own free will."

Pat was approaching the office.

"Well, officer, you back?"

"I am back, Pat."

"You may go, Pearson. I will send for you when I need you."

"And if you knew all I know, you would need him now, before he went."

"Well, Pat, have you done anything with Prisoner 78?"

"I? No, sirree; he is a 'fellow'—a pet around here, he is."

"What do you mean, Pat—a 'fellow,' 'pet'?"

"Well, your honor, I never was a tell-tale, and I don't want to begin now."

"Do you know anything, Pat, that I should know?"

"I think if you knew all I do; you would have another prisoner in here to feed."

"I have always trusted you, Pat. Can not you now trust me?"

"Sure, I can trust you, but what about the other fellow. Can I trust him?"

"I will take care of that part of it if you will tell me what you know, Pat."

"I am going to think it over myself a while. I don't like to report too many times, for fear I don't get it the same each time."

"You may not have to repeat, Pat."

"I hope not, for I feel sorry for the poor man, to think he has no feeling."

"You would just as well tell all you know. I am investigating, as it is, and I think along those lines, and 'murder will out,' you know."

"And some things will out themselves, as well as murder."

"Pat, in justice to yourself, you will have to tell me what you know. Here comes Pearson. I will hear what you have to say later. You may go."

"I am going to remain on guard to-night, officer, and I shall not be in the office. I speak of this so that you will not keep late hours for me."

"Very well, Pearson."

"I wonder what he is up to now," thought the superintendent. "I must be on guard myself to-night, and I must remain where I can watch cell No. 78. It is now ten-thirty o'clock—a good hour to lock up the office. I'll walk quietly to cell 77—it is empty to-night—and I may know more in the morning than I do to-night. Here comes Pat. I will tell him to keep watch on the office to-night, for emergency calls. He can hear the bells ringing, and if—well, by George! I'd rather Pat would not know where I am. I'll have to take the chances of the bells ringing. I may hear them if they do. It is not a great distance to the office."

"Your honor, I'm thinking of going to my bed. I am top-heavy, and would like to lay me down for a while. I think it would do me good. Too much to carry around, and too good to let it get away."

"All right, Pat; you may go."

To himself: "Now I shall learn something for myself. I'd better disguise myself, for fear of meeting Pearson. I'll put on this slouch hat. He would not recognize me in that; a hat changes one's looks sometimes so that even close friends could not be recognized.

"Hark! I hear voices! I believe it is Pearson's voice in cell 78. I must be very quiet. Sure enough! Now I shall find out for myself."

"I will try, Clarence, to favor you in having you placed in a position where you can make your get-away, and I will give you money to go on. Would you go if that opportunity presented itself?"

"Oliver, what do you mean? Are you trying to get me here for the rest of my life? I would not be here at all if you would do for me what a brother should do."

"I am trying to help you, Clarence, and you won't let me."

"I don't want your help, if I have to get it in that way. Why don't you do unto me as you would have me do to you?"

"I have a family and they are in society, and I am not so free to go as you are, and if this comes out, I may have to remain here, but not by choice."

"Can't you see the trouble I'm in?"

"I can see if you would get out of here and they could not find you, then they would drop it all, and you would be a free man and so would I."

"If I were to do as you want me to, where could I go and what could I do? I have no money."

"Did I not say that I would help you? You can leave the city and I will send you money under an assumed name. I can take care of you."

"You are looking out for yourself, I know, Oliver. If you had not stolen all my part of the estate, you would not be here this hour of the night, talking to me. You have no brotherly love for me, or you would get me out and prove to the world that I am innocent, and take me to your comfortable home as a long-lost brother. I would not disgrace your society family. My mother was a good woman, and if I did fail to get the education I should have received, I have a good, pure heart in me, and am one that has always tried to do right and will do so as long as I live. It is not always the one, Oliver, who had the advantages, who has the best education, that is the purest. I am at fault for not having an education, I know, for I ran away from home when I was a boy, but I have never committed a crime, as you have done."

"You are not looking at this as you should. I am going to say to you that if you fail to do as you promised me you would—if you do not deny your name—I will murder you."

"Then you would murder me for wealth and society, would you, Oliver?"

"I would."

"Then what would you do? You could not enjoy either."

"I might say you were disobedient and that I had to kill you. You know how much trouble you have caused since you were here, and it would be no trouble for me to get out of it. So, this is your warning. Now remember, I am leaving you for the last time, to think this over, and I want your answer to-day. It will soon be daylight. I must not be seen in your cell. Think this over well."

"And so, my brother threatens to kill me if I do not commit a crime! And I must think this over and let him know to-day! Well, I could let him know now. I will not leave these prison walls without the proper orders, and I am afraid to say as much to him," said the prisoner aloud. "What shall I do? To tell what he has done would mean a term for him in this very prison, and not to tell means death to me. Oh! what shall I do? Pray? Yes, pray that dear mother will come to me and help me; that she will not allow her honored son to murder her dishonored son, as he threatened to do. He said that mother mourned me as dead. Oh, if I had only died before all this happened! I am going to pray for help from her now—not for material help; I do not want any money or sympathy in poverty, I only want help from Heaven to know what to do. I shall kneel on this cold, hard floor and pray.

"Father above, I am not a murderer, as Thou knowest. I ask forgiveness for the sins that I have committed, for we all sin, though often unintentionally. O Father in Heaven, I ask that the spirit of my dear mother may be allowed to return to earth and watch over me, that her son Cain may not slay Abel. And, O dear Father, I am here for another's crime, as Thou, blessed Father, knowest. I pray that I may be helped—not to be freed from here until it is proved to the world that I am innocent. I feel my dear mother's presence near me. Oh, how grateful I am! Now, dear Father, give me help to show the one who has given me so short a time to pray the right way. The time is near when I must decide between life and death. Thou knowest best. I trust Thee to look after me in this hour of need. And, O dear Father, help my brother, that he may know and do the right. Forgive him, Father, and lead him. Go with each of us in our humble way. May we ever feel Thy presence near us. May holy angels hover around us and help and comfort us in this time of need. May we feel their presence. I ask this from a heart filled with faith, hope, and love. Amen."

The trembling voice was silent. The heart of the superior officer went out in sympathy to the poor, abused convict who had the strength to resist temptation, and who could yet forgive his selfish, wicked brother.

CHAPTER XV
"Thank God, He Is Innocent!"

"Well, I have been repaid for this night's work. I must get back to the office, before I am seen coming from this cell," said the official.

"Good morning, sir."

"Good morning, Pearson. You are looking tired. Have you had a hard night of it?"

"Yes; I am trying to unravel a mystery, and I am somewhat worried."

"So am I, Pearson. I am trying to look into the past life of this prisoner, No. 78. I want to see if he has been a bad fellow. I am under the impression that he is not guilty of the crime for which he is being punished; he seems so honest about his past, and he has even given his real name, and that is some proof that he is no crook, or murderer. He would surely deny his name if he were either, and I feel it my duty to look into this whole affair."

"Well, officer, I am under the impression that he has registered under an assumed name—that he is holding back his real name."

"Why have you formed such an impression?"

"Well, I have a feeling that he will tell his real name if pressed to do so."

"I will send for him and we can press him for the truth."

Pat's voice was heard as he approached, saying: "I wonder what this day will bring forth. Here I am, walking to the office. I have a feeling that it is time the 'pet-fellow' had a little exercise, and I must be there in case I'm needed."

"There you are, Pat. You are always on hand when you are needed. You may bring No. 78 into the office."

"I am getting to be a fortune-teller indeed. I can tell when I am wanted without being told. Here, you 'pet-fellow'! Wake up! I am going to take you for your morning's walk."

"I am very willing to go."

"I am quite sure that you will go, willing or not. When I am told to do anything, I usually do it. Here we are."

"Bring him in, Pat."

"Please open the door. How do you expect me to do—break in?"

"The night lock is thrown on, officer. How did that happen? We never do so unless we all go inside of the prison. Were you in the prison last night?"

"We will discuss that later. We have sent for the prisoner and he is here. Let him in."

"You may go, Pat. We have some investigations to make, and we prefer to be alone."

Pat went, out, remaining within hearing and saying: "Here is a very comfortable seat. I will sit myself down and I won't have to walk so far when I come back."

"Now, did I understand you—No. 78 I am speaking to—did I understand you to say that you have given your real Christian name, and surname also, to be recorded in the prison books?"

"Well, I have been thinking."

"About changing your name?"

"How do you know that, sir?"

"Mr. Pearson has told me so."

"He told you so?"

"Do you deny it—can you, will you?"

"My God! what shall I do? You have told him all?"

"I have told him nothing."

"Pearson, why are you so excited?"

"I am astonished at your falsehood."

"And you may be more astonished before I get through with you.

"Come, did I understand you to say—or have you answered me? Do you hear me speak to you?"

"I do, sir. Well, then, I will have to be protected if I tell the truth."

"From whom?"

"Oh, man! can not you see the danger I am in:"

"You in danger? Explain in what way. With your God, for swearing to falsehoods, or from your fellow-man?"

"I have not deceived my God."

"Then you have given your own real name?"

"I will tell you. I have."

"So, you want protection, now you have told the truth? Give me the name of your enemy."

"Officer, can you not relieve me of this torture? Can you not see?"

"Yes, I think I can.

"Well, Pearson, do you think you could rest comfortably behind the bars for a few hours?"

"I? What do you mean?"

"I mean that you have been trying to bribe this man to disown his name. Now I am not in the dark. I understand it all, and I am going to make a clean breast of it. I shall send him back to his cell, and send you to another one."

"I'll just get up and stretch myself. I may have to use my muscles, and club too," commented Pat. "I hope he will like his new home."

"You must have good hearing, Pat," said the official. "I was just going to ring for you. You must hear my thoughts. You may take No. 78 back, and return at once."

"I will, your honor.

"Walk up fast, 'pet.' I am going to fill the order to a minute, and I will sure be proud to see him leaving me alone for a while. Here we are. Get in gently, 'pet.' I'll be closing the door easy, to not shock you. Now I must be bating it back to the office to get the other man."

"Well, Pearson, 'murder will out.'"

"I have not murdered anyone, and why should you talk to me in that way?"

"I don't think that your brother has, either."

"My brother!"

"Yes, your brother. Do you not know that the convict is your brother? If you do not, I do."

"We have the same name. Is that any reason why we should be brothers?"

"Not because you have the same name, no; but in this case the two men who bear the same name are brothers."

"Tell me, why am I to be placed behind the bars?"

"So that you may not kill your brother."

"Man! I'm not going behind the bars on any such freak ideas as yours. I shall not be disgraced by a prisoner who has no cause to fear me, just because he has a name like mine and makes the statement that he fears me."

"You understand it all. Pearson, here is Pat. You may occupy cell No. 77, next to that of your brother.

"Come along, Pat. Take charge of Mr. Pearson, here.

"Give me your arms, officer."

"I will never do so, not as long as I have a drop of blood in my body. I shall not give up my arms and allow Pat, the scoundrel, to place me behind the bars."

"You will have it to do, sir. I will see that you do. Hand them over to me."

"I refuse to do so. I will die before I do."

"Well, me friend, you had better ask your God about that. Perhaps you are a little perverse about going."

"You are not acting wisely, Pearson. You had just as well be brave and await the outcome."

"Message here," called out a voice.

"Give it to me. The charges? None? Very well."

He read: "Your answer is, 'Yes; we have the man in jail. Have his confession of murder of woman.'"

"My God! Can it be? He has received it, and my brother will be free."

"I have not been deceived. Thank God, he is innocent!" exclaimed the superintendent.

CHAPTER XVI
A New Prisoner in Cell 78

"Mr. Pearson, have you decided to go quietly? I think you may now occupy your brother's cell, since he is innocent of the crime, and the real murderer has confessed. This is the telegram which brought the news."

"Perhaps if I would call him a 'pet' and 'fellow,' he would come along with me," said Pat. "The officer requested me to take you, so here, you 'pet-fellow,' you must go."

"Pat, Pat, don't kill him! Let him up! I think he will go."

"I think he will, too. Here, take his gun—no, perhaps I had better take it along. I may need two of them. I only have six cartridges, and I have been carrying them some time. I may get a chance now to get rid of them, and I may need more."

"Pat, get some water. I'm afraid you have killed him."

"Well, he said he would die before he would go, and devil take him if he wanted to rush off in a hurry."

"I see his mouth twitch. I hope he will revive soon."

"I think he is saying to himself what he will do when he gets up, but if I have any strength left, I think he will come along with me, as soon as he is able to walk, and nary stretcher will I carry him on, until I know he is invade a dead one. He went to fight back. I think when he comes to, he will see that fighting is hard on the eyes. See the eye turn black, will you? You would think he had been dead a long while and was mortifying."

"Come, Pat, help me to get him on his feet."

"You had better let him rest easy where he is."

"I am asking you for help, and I want it."

"I'll help you, your honor. I never have refused a thing you have asked me to do."

"Come, Pearson; can you stand up? Try."

"I am not hurt. I am only dizzy."

"I am glad. I hope that you will now obey orders, and not cause any more excitement."

"What shall I do, officer?"

"Pat, show him the way."

"Come along, officer—Mr. Pearson—'pet' 'fellow.' Oh, how I would like to add a few more pet names to them! Indeed, when he has no gun, he is willing to ask what to do. Well, I will show you. This way out. I feel that you was not so very much surprised, only in the one way."

"So, the poor fellow was innocent, and the guilty one has confessed. I hope I shall never have another innocent man here while I am in charge of the place. I must send word to Pearson's family. They will be alarmed when he does not come home. It will be a great shock to the family—to those beautiful society daughters. It will be a calamity to them. How shall I break the news? I would not dare to send Pat. He has a grievance against Pearson, and would not show any mercy on the family. I shall call the officials together and state the whole circumstances, and then we can see what steps to take to protect his family. I am anxious to see Pat back. I hope he will not have any more trouble. Here he comes now. Well, Pat, is he all right?"

"I think he is able to talk. After he was locked up, I stepped to one side and he thought I had gone, and the poor brother was getting the devil, and he promised him more than I just now gave him. I think that the poor brother will be scared to leave the place when he is turned loose."

"Pat, why are you referring to the brother? What do you know about it?"

"I guess what I know would do someone good and would bring someone harm."

"Tell me, Pat, how did you hear these things?"

"I have not got these ears on the sides of my head just for looks. They was put there to hear with, and I am going to hear when there is anything to be heard."

"When did you hear all this, Pat?"

"I am after hearing it some time ago."

"Pat, I thought I could trust you to tell me everything that went wrong inside of these prison walls."

"Faith, and you can, and I would of told you if it was wrong, your honor, but I thought it was all right if he is guilty of staling all the money, he ought to be punished, and I did not think it necessary to tell you. I expected to find out what he did with the money. Maybe the poor fellow could get it back."

"You have a secret, Pat, and you must tell me all about it."

"Well, I have got to tell it some time, and if I tell it now, I will have to tell it over again, so what is the use of telling it twice?"

"I believe it is something I should know now, and perhaps I do know, but not exactly what you do."

"If I tell you now, I may not tell it the same way the next time, and if you only hear anything once, you will always think that is right, and if you hear it twice and not alike, then 'you have not told the truth' is the first thing you are accused of."

"Well, Pat, that is right; but can not you remember how to tell it both times the same way?"

"Yes, this 'pen' is holding three or four poor devils to-day for not remembering and telling it alike both times."

"I will let you think it over, Pat. Try to make up your mind to remember as you heard it. You may go now, and see if Mr. Pearson is all right. Report within the next half-hour."

"Now if he is all right, do you want me to report now, or wait the half-hour?"

"Pat, if anything is wrong, let me know at once."

"That I will, your honor."

"Now Pat is gone, I must let the family know, and I think I should let them know at once, for I may not be able to get the officials together as soon as I should like to. I will risk it and call them over the wires, and try to explain some minor part to them, so they will know something is wrong. I can say that he had some trouble with one of the prisoners, as he has a black eye that Pat gave him. No, that won't do. They would ask why I was holding him behind the bars if he had trouble. That has often happened and the officers are compelled to subdue the unruly prisoners, but they do not get locked up for it. I shall have to say something. When you try to fix up something, you never get it said just as you had it fixed up, so I'll get them on the wire and trust to saying the right thing.

"Central, give me Main 505, please.

"Hello! Is this Mrs. Pearson? Mrs. Pearson, I have something to say to you. I should like you to come to the office at once. No, I hardly have time to tell you over the 'phone. Very well. Good-bye.

"What did I say? I was so nervous I hardly knew. I don't like to tell the family about the head of the household. I think that he could explain better himself. I really don't know just what I did say. I think I did not tell them how bad things were. By George! I believe that is Mrs. Pearson coming—and the beautiful daughters too. It is. Did I tell her to come? Yes, and here comes Pat with Pearson. My God! has he had trouble with him again? He is covered with blood."

"Your honor, here he is. Everything was all right when I went around, but the chap got smart and I have been bating him for a half-hour, then the time was up and you said report, and here I am with what is left of him. I hear a knock on the door.

"Come right in, ladies.

"Officer, here."

"Oh, papa, papa!"

"My dear husband! What has happened to you?"

Pat muttered: "Only a good bating, and he deserved it."

"Pat, I must censure you for speaking in that way. I did not intend that you should open the door, and I intended to place him in the second room. I had no chance to speak to you before you opened the door. Now you may go."

"I will, your honor. You always told me to open the door when you heard a knock. Now you blame me for it. How do I know what to do and do it right?"

Outside, Pat whispered to himself: "I have had quite a time and feel pretty tired. I don't think I will go, for I have a knowledge-place here where I get all my news, and I think I will get some more knowledge and sit myself down for a while. What the deuce is all of the crying for inside? I know I did not bate him to death."

"My dear madam, calm yourself. I will explain the best I can. I hardly know how to do so. I think Mr. Pearson could do better than I could."

"Mother, take papa home. Do, please, out of this horrid place, never to return."

"I am very sorry, miss, but I—"

"You do not expect my husband to remain on duty when he is suffering, do you?

"Tell me how did you get so badly hurt," said Mrs. Pearson, turning to her husband.

"Mother, do you not see that he can not raise his head?"

Pat, listening outside, remarked: "Not because he is hurt, little miss, but because he is ashamed to raise his head, and I am afraid you will not be able to raise your head up when this is all brought out. I feel I would of done the poor fellow a favor if I had beat him to death. Ho will have to die sometime, and perhaps this would of suited him better."

"He will have to remain in the hospital, here, and we will take care of him."

"Oh! I have a doctor, my family doctor, and I want him to look after him. What did you send for me for? Wasn't it to take him home?" said Mrs. Pearson.

"No; I did not know at the time I was talking that he was injured. You know, he had this trouble—I told Pat to call around to his cell and see how he was getting along."

"His cell! his cell!"

"Yes, my wife and dear children, I am a prisoner here. I can not go home with you."

"Papa! oh, papa!"

"You a prisoner here? What have you done to be confined in this place, a prisoner?"

"I can not tell you. Go home. I may never get the chance again."

"You a prisoner? My husband, whom I have promised to honor, a criminal? The father of my children a criminal? Oh, no! I do not believe it."

"Madam, I think you had better take your daughters home. Calm yourself, and I will explain all to you later."

"I can not leave this place without my husband."

Pat, listening, said: "Another boarder. I know she will object to the kind of service she will get here, and the linen napkin. I think she will change her mind, and I hope she will change it now and not shed any more tears. I'm a hard-hearted Irishman, and could bate a fellow to death, but when it comes to hearing the dear ladies cry, I am finding myself dropping a tear myself."

"Oh, papa! tell us what you have done."

"Daughter, I have deceived you all these years, and I can do so no longer. I will tell you now. Be brave, and listen. I was one of the two sons my dear mother bore, and my brother, when a small boy, ran away from home. We never heard from him, and I thought he was dead, as did my dear mother. Many years afterward my poor mother died, broken-hearted over her lost son, and I had to swear to falsehood to obtain the estate. I swore that I knew he was dead, and so got all of the estate. What to do after I had received it, I did not know. I thought to invest it would be to double the amount. Instead of that, I lost all except what I had when I married your mother. Now the lost brother is found in this prison, and I am an embezzler. Now I must suffer for the rest of my days."

"You have carried that secret in your heart all these years, and I, your wife, did not know it? You deceived me, and now bring disgrace upon your daughters?"

"Oh, mother! can you not see that papa is punished enough? Do not torture him any more," said one of the daughters.

"I will disown my father if he has committed a crime like that," said the other one.

"Sister," returned the first, "he is not at fault. Do not speak to him in that way. You and I are his only children, and we must not do as those two brothers did, drift apart. We must not make the same mistake."

CHAPTER XVII
DESERTED

"Gertie, I will not allow you to compare yourself and your sister with what could happen. I am like daughter Amelia. I am not going to forgive him—no, not I. I shall return to my home and feel very uncomfortable in it, after knowing how it was obtained. Come, my daughters."

"I shall return, papa," said Gertie, "and see you. I shall always love you, for you have been a good father to me. You gave me my education and provided instruction in music. No one can take that away from me. I shall always remember you and love you and I shall do all that I can for you in times to come. Good-bye, dear papa. Do not weep. Mother and sister can never turn my love from you. If I ever can redeem your good name for you, I shall be repaid for all, and I hope and pray that I shall be able to do so."

"Gertie, you have said enough to your convict father. Come at once. We must leave this horrid place, never to return. Come, come, daughters."

Addressing her husband, the wife said: "You got in this trouble without your family's assistance, and you can get out the same way."

"Oh, mother! do not talk so cruelly to papa. I know his heart is broken. I am sure that he believed himself right when he made the statement that his brother was dead. He did not dream that his brother was alive, or that he would ever hear of him again."

"Gertie, go along with your mother. I will suffer alone."

"I will share it with you, papa. Good-bye."

"Mr. Pearson, I shall place you in the second room here, and I shall call in the officials for consultation and see what can be done. I regret very much to have to do so, but it is my duty."

"I am a prisoner here, and shall obey your rules. I will step inside. You may take me in. I shall not cause you any unnecessary trouble."

"Well, I have got a job, to turn the key on the gentleman. I'll just step in. I feel I have saved myself a good many steps by finding myself a resting-place so near." It was Pat, talking to himself.

"I was just turning to call for you, Pat."

"Well, I am here."

"You may see that water is in the room for Pearson, then lock the door."

"I will do that, your honor, with pleasure. Where is the man to occupy the room?"

"He has stepped in there, Pat."

"Very obliging, he is. I think that bating did him some good.

"Here is some water for you, sir, and if you want anything, call me. Or have I given you all you wanted me to—faith, I mane in the way of a bating?

"The poor fellow sits there with his head down as though I had never said a word to him, so I'll lock him in and let him slape it off."

"Pat, I am going to call in the high officials to-day, and I want you to be present; I am going to call on you for some of your knowledge."

"How in the devil do you know where my knowledge-place is? You may have it all and I will find me another resting-place."

"Pat, you do not understand me. I meant that you must tell what you know about this Pearson and his brother. Explain what you mean by giving me all the place of knowledge."

"Well, your honor, you see I have been wanted here and there so many times I found myself a resting-place outside of this office, so I could be here when you wanted me—and when you didn't want me."

"Do you call that a 'knowledge-place'? I should call it a 'resting-place.'"

"I rested while I was getting my knowledge."

"You were reading, were you?"

"Devil a bit did I read."

"How, then, did you get your knowledge?"

"Well, if you have things that you try to keep from hearing—and indeed I tried to keep from hearing the poor family crying, I was dropping a few tears myself—then—"

"You heard the conversation, did you?"

"I don't know if that is what you call it, but I don't care to hear any more of it; the last time I felt the way I did was when the only friend I ever had died, and that was me dog. I never had a poor father or mother—if I did, they never told me about it; but one kind lady told the good woman that raised me I was too small to know me father and mother, so I don't know any, and if I had any—God bless 'em!—

their son never had to swear all the children was dead to get what the old folks left."

"Pat, you have heard all about this, have you?"

"I don't know what 'this' is. You mean have I heard something about this poor man's troubles?"

"Here are the officials, now. You may go. I shall send for you."

"I am glad I can go. I am not going to meet the high officials. They might be so high I couldn't make myself heard. I'll just sit myself down."

"Good morning, gentlemen."

"Good morning." "Good morning."

"Why have we been called?"

"Mr. McHenry, there has been trouble here in regard to one of the prisoners who is a very poor man. Strange things have happened since he has been in the prison, and the strangest part of all is that he is a brother of Officer Pearson."

"A brother of Officer Pearson?"

"The man was convicted of murder on circumstantial evidence."

"Of murder—a brother of Officer Pearson!"

"Yes. I'll explain further. I have a telegram here, stating that the real murderer has confessed."

"Well, I am glad. I hope that his brother is not a murderer. I have a high regard for Officer Pearson."

"Gentlemen, the worst is yet to come. Mr. Pearson is himself under lock and key."

"I dare say you are telling the truth."

"I am, sir. He was heard trying to bribe his brother to swear falsely—to deny his own name."

"Pray, what was that for?"

"I regret to say that he has swindled his brother out of his part of the estate by swearing the brother was dead. By doing this, Mr. Pearson fell heir to the entire estate, which was large, and he lost it all, except the home which his family now occupies."

"The poor man! What was the amount?"

"In the hundreds of thousands."

"Well, well! How sorry I am to hear that about Mr. Pearson!"

"You have not heard all yet about Mr. Pearson. I am going to explain it all. He threatened to kill his brother if he did not swear that he had been registered under an assumed name. In that way Pearson hoped not to be recognized as the convict's brother."

"You are relating something that can be verified, are you?"

"I am."

"Where did you get your information?"

"I have a very trustworthy guard that overheard some things."

"You are not believing all these things from hearsay, are you?"

"I have heard enough myself to be convinced that Mr. Pearson is guilty."

"Call Mr. Pearson in."

"Well, here is where I bring in the fellow with the black eye. I'll just step to the door, by accident," said Pat, outside.

"Pat, step in and show Mr. Pearson in."

"I will, your honor."

"Oh! you have him in there, have you, locked up?"

"I believe I mentioned the fact that I had him under lock and key."

"My god, man, what have you done to this poor man?"

"Mr. Pearson, I am sorry to see this."

Pat muttered in a low voice: "You would be doing a good turn if you would go to the poor wife and give some sympathy to those beautiful daughters. They have never stole anything and threatened to kill afterwards if the one they robbed hollered about it. I have given him a good bating, and I think it did him good, but I never want the ladies to come here again and do any more crying. I had to drop a tear myself."

"Officer, what does this mean? Did you allow that Irishman to beat this poor man like this before his family?"

"No, sir; his family were not here."

"He spoke of their tears."

"They were here afterward, and—"

"Go on and tell what happened. I am astonished."

"I have explained what he did. I do not see why, as he has violated the law, he should not be locked up as any other prisoner is."

"A man is not guilty until proved so."

"And I order this man to be turned loose. You have no authority to claim him as a prisoner. He has never been arrested, no warrant for him has been issued, and I do not believe him guilty."

"I am in a position to prove his guilt."

"I do not believe you, sir."

"I shall ask Pearson to speak for himself."

"You—Mr. Pearson I am speaking to—please tell the officials here what you told your wife and daughters."

"I am willing to plead guilty."

"Oh, my God! And my son to marry a daughter of this man! I can not allow him to do so. Take Pearson away—take him away and do what you please with him. I have heard enough from his own lips—'I plead guilty.'"

"Come, McHenry, I have had nothing to say, and now I do not want to say anything. I have heard enough."

"This is awful. My son to marry this man's daughter! The engagement was announced last night. The marriage shall never take place."

"Come along, Mr. McHenry. We can talk that over after we leave here."

"Good morning, sir."

"Good morning, gentlemen."

"Well, Pat, you may place the prisoner in cell 77."

"Come along. You are a fine bird, you are. You are not satisfied with ruining your own reputation, but you had to bring sorrow to your daughter. Your children must suffer along with yourself. I pity the poor young man that is engaged to marry the girl. I have been there myself. I was engaged to a beautiful girl, and when the father found out some things he would never listen to me marrying her, and it was not because I stole all the money I could lay me hands on; it was because I was an Irishman.

"Well, you have got a nice place here. 'Tis a pity you had not been here all the time, then you would have had all your money yet.

"I'll drop around male times, and see if you have the same as the other gentlemen get here."

"I am not fully decided what to do," said the superintendent. "I must write at once and acknowledge the receipt of this telegram, and I must see that the proper authorities get the confession of this man Pearson, and place him where he should be. And if Clarence is proved innocent, he ought to be freed at once.

"I hear a faint knock. I hope that it is not Pearson's wife. I must open the door. They know that I am here at this hour of the day.

"Good morning, Miss Gertie."

"I have brought papa something to eat. I had such a hard time to get this for him. Mother and sister went shopping, and while they were gone, I did some baking and brought it to papa. May I see him?"

"I will see that your father gets it, Miss Gertie. If you are in a hurry to return before your mother and sister get home, you had better go at once."

"Oh, no! I want to see papa. I want to tell him something. Is he not in this room where he was before?"

"Well, no—I—had—to use that room, and I gave him another room. I think that he is asleep now. He had a very restless night. I feel that he should not be disturbed."

"Officer, I must see him. I want to tell him something. I have a secret to tell him—not exactly a secret, but it is to papa, perhaps."

"I am sorry, but I shall have to deliver the message for you. I am worthy of your confidence. I do feel very sorry for you and your father. Pray trust me with the secret. I'll deliver it as it is given to me."

"Officer, I am heart-broken. I do want to see papa."

"I think I have him where I can put me hand on him, and I hope I'll never have to put me club on him again, for I feel sorry every time I hear the daughter cry. Poor girl! I hope she won't come here again. If she does, I hope she will lave the tears at home, for every time I hear her cry, I think of me poor dog," said Pat, outside. "I'll be going along by the office and see if I'm wanted."

"Here comes Pat. I'll have him bring your father in, if he is not asleep.

"Pat, save yourself the bother of coming in, and go and see if Mr. Pearson is awake. If so, tell him I want to see him."

"Mr. Guard—Pat, please bring papa. If he is asleep, waken him and tell him that I am here."

"I was in hopes the poor girl would not come again, but here she is, and bring him in I will. It's the first time in me life anyone called me by the handle to me name. It's always 'Pat,' but she called me 'Mr. Pat.' I'd do anything for the girl. I'd even treat the father nice. Poor man, maybe, after all, he really thought his brother was dead.

"Mr. Pearson, your honor, will you please come along with me, and oblige me? Your beautiful daughter is in the office and wants to tell you something."

"Pat, I do not care to see her. I know how the poor girl will feel to leave me, and if she does not see me, it will not be so hard on her nor on me."

"I wish you would come. She is waiting for you, and indeed, I'd be disobeying orders to go back without you, and I don't want to take you, as I have done."

"I will go, then. Pat, you talk like a good sort of a fellow, after all, and I'll go peacefully with you."

"Thank you, sir. This is a wise man."

"Miss Gertie, we have visiting rules. I will give you this card, and you can see the days we have for company."

"Oh, Mr. Officer! could I not come any time? You know I have to watch for my chance to get away. I could not see papa often enough."

"Now, you may step in and talk with your daughter. I have some very important business to take care of."

"Pat, come around soon again. I may need you to take some mail to the train, as I am anxious to have the letters go at once."

"Well, I may as well sit myself down and get some more knowledge. I hope I will not hear any crying. Poor girl, how she did rush to her papa and kiss him! If I had a daughter to kiss me, I would fall dead," mused Pat.

"Oh, papa, I am so glad I could come and bring you something to eat! Mother and sister were out shopping and I found the opportunity to bring this to you. And I so wanted to bring you some news. Papa, you know Amelia is going to marry Clyde McHenry? Oh, papa, you are so pale! Are you ill?"

"Daughter, I fear the marriage will never take place."

"Why, papa? The engagement was announced last night, and the date set six weeks from then. Would you object, papa?"

"No, daughter; I would not interfere with the marriage, but—but—"

"Well, papa, what do you want to say?"

"It will all be known soon enough, and the dear girl will suffer, I know."

"Oh, dear papa, don't cry so hard! I am trying to be brave for you, and I want you to for me—and Amelia will be happy."

"Well, if the man isn't crying! It's not enough to hear the ladies, and when the men begin, I'll have to move on, I think. I have enough knowledge for to last the rest of me life," muttered Pat.

"Pat, you may take this letter to the train. Pat, you are wanted. I wonder if he has forgot his orders."

"Oh, the devil take you! I'm coming, as soon as I get these tears all out of me eyes," mumbled Pat. Then aloud: "Yes, I'm coming. What can I do for you?"

"Mail this letter on the morning train. Do not delay getting it off.

"Miss Gertie, I shall have to ask you if you have visited long enough with your father?" said the superintendent.

CHAPTER XVIII
Pat's Temptation

"I am very thankful to you, sir. I shall visit papa soon again. I hope that I may be allowed to see him any time when I can get away. You see, sister is making arrangements for her marriage, to take place in six weeks, and she and mother will be away from home at different times. I could then hurry and come to see papa, and please, officer, could I be admitted at any time?"

"Miss Gertie, I should like to grant you the privilege, but I fear I can not do so. I am sworn to follow prison rules."

"Oh, how cruel! To know that I could not be allowed the pleasure—the only pleasure I have—of seeing my father!"

"I am very sorry. I would help you to do anything possible without violating the prison rules."

"Dear child, go now. You must, as you know that we are not obeying orders, and I am very thankful for the pleasure the officer has given us—to see each other. I want you to thank him and go."

"Papa, I did thank him, and will again. Oh! if I only knew that I could return often to see you, I could go more contentedly. Good-bye, dear papa. Do not worry, papa; I shall always be your Gertie, and a dutiful daughter.

"Good-bye. I thank you, officer."

"Mr. Pearson, you have a beautiful daughter," said the superintendent as the girl passed out; "not only in looks, but she is good and loyal to her father. How proud I should be of a daughter like her!"

"I am proud of her. And I am ashamed to think that I have brought on her this disgrace. I feel that I shall never again be able to hold up my head, if I should get out of here."

"Do not talk like that. We can live down disgrace and you can show the world that you are not a bad man, after all, at heart, and I don't think you are, Pearson."

"Well, I'm glad I made the train all right," said Pat, "and I got the letter off. I feel better now—not so ornery. I will take me time going back. What do I see? The dear little girl that called me name with the handle on it? And I do believe she is crying. Now, I can't stand to pass her and see her shedding tears. What could I say to comfort her? Well, if I don't say any more than 'howdy,' it will help some.

"How do you do?"

"Oh, dear! I was not looking up, and I didn't see you."

"I know you didn't see me, but I saw you, and I want to speak to you, for sympathy's sake."

"I thank you, Mr. Pat. I am so sad to think I can not see papa often. I can not get away always on the visiting days, and would have to come when I could find the opportunity."

"Well, I will see if you can not get in when you come."

"Oh, no! you are very kind, but the officer in charge said that he was sworn to do his duty, and the rules of the prison are, 'No visitors except on visiting day.' I shall have to come when I can get away on visiting days."

"Well, I hope to be able to break the rules."

"You must not do so on my account, or make any attempt to do so, Mr. Pat."

"What could I say next?" thought Pat.

"I will be looking for you if you will say when you will call to see your father again."

"I do not know that I could come when I would plan to do so—if I could come on the days set aside for visitors."

"Well, may I ask how I could help you?"

"I do not know now. I thank you. Oh, yes! please be kind to papa, won't you, please, Mr. Pat?"

"That I will, indeed! I will, and I will see that he has plenty to eat and drink. Now I must move on back to me job. Good-bye."

"He has promised to look after papa, and I shall be so grateful to him for his kindness—shown to my dear, heart-broken father. I will beg my mother again, when she has relented toward me, to let me visit my dear papa on the right days. What pleasure I shall have, looking forward to the times when I may see him, if mother will only consent!"

"Pat, you back? I think it has taken you a long time to go to the train and back. Why the delay?"

"Well, your honor, I am back and ready to do anything you want me to."

"You may see that Mr. Pearson is locked in cell 77."

"Mr. Pearson, will you kindly come along with me? I am not doing this as a pleasure, but as my sworn duty."

"Pat, I understand your position. I know I had to do many things I did not like to do, but I understand the prison rules, and I'll obey orders."

"You will please step in here, Mr. Pearson. I am going to see that you have plenty to eat and drink. That I promised your daughter."

"You promised my daughter? When did you have the opportunity to talk to her? I have been in her presence each time and all of the time when she was here, and she has visited me only twice."

"Faith, and did you not hear the officer ask me why the delay? Well, as I was coming back from the train, I met your daughter, and she was feeling bad, and I felt sorry for her and tried to comfort her the best I could, and I bade the time of day to her."

"Was that all of the conversation you had?"

"No, sir; I asked the poor, heart-broken girl if I could do anything for her, and the only thing I could do to help her I couldn't do, but I offered to try, but she shook her head and said, 'No, indeed.' She don't take after you for honesty."

"Pat, what was the help you offered her?"

"You understand the same as myself that the rules here don't allow visiting only on visiting days, and the girl said she couldn't always get away on visiting days."

"What could you help her to do, Pat?"

"I thought, perhaps, I could change the rule."

"Pat, you are a good fellow, and I do not know how to thank you for all of your kindness."

"Wait a minute. I don't need any thanking for bating you. I got me spite off you then."

"I wonder what is keeping Pat so long," thought the superintendent. "Did I tell him to return? I do not believe I did. Well, I'll throw the lock on and step around and see if I can see him near. I will just walk toward the new prisoner's cell, and perhaps I may meet Pat.

"Almost there, and I do not see him? I'll just step up and look inside cell 77.

"What do I hear? Pat's voice inside? I must find out what this means."

"Pat, you have had a hard time all your life, working, haven't you?" said the prisoner.

"Me b'y," returned Pat, "I never knew anything but work."

"Well, Pat, don't you think that a man would be foolish to work if he could live without it?"

"Indeed, I do."

"Pat, would you like to live without working if you had a chance?"

"I would be a gentleman if I could. They was always something about a man that did not work I rather admired, and wondered how they felt, dressed up all the time."

"Pat, if you had the chance, you would try it, wouldn't you?"

"Well, faith, and I think I would."

"Pat, you understand what I'm here for?"

"Faith, and I don't want to be here for the same purpose you are, to be a gentleman, or to be an officer as you was."

"No, that was by choice, Pat, I was here. I have plenty of money, and now it will do me no good, if I am to stay in here, and if I were out of here, I would have enough to last us both the rest of our lives. Now, Pat, can you find a way to get me away from here, so this place will never see nor hear of either of us again?"

"Well, me friend, what would be the job I would have after we got away from here?"

"Did I not tell you that you would never have to work any more?"

"And I would be a gentleman, then?"

"Yes, you would, Pat. Now, let me plan this. You are trusted, and the superintendent has confidence in you, and you can get me out of here, and walk out yourself, and then we can leave the country together."

"And what would the poor man do without me help?"

"Oh, go along! What does he care for your help? There are many others who would be glad to take your place, and you would be a gentleman then, Pat. Just think of it!"

"Well, I can't think of a gentleman in me, as I never was one."

"Of course, you always had to work, but you will never have to if you get me away from here. Come, Pat, wake up! You may never have the chance again to be a gentleman."

"I will study this over and see if I want this chance. I feel the cold chills run up and down me back. Does that belong to the appearance of a gentleman?"

"It does. You see, just talking about it, you are feeling the gentleman vibrations."

"Well, I think I have got the plot, and what I miss now I can get along without. I will hasten to the office," the superintendent whispered.

Pat continued: "I think I'll be getting along back to the office, Mr. Pearson. The superintendent will be after asking me, 'Why the delay?'"

"Come around often, Pat, and talk to me."

"That I will. Well, I am a gentleman, or can be if I want to give up me job here."

"Pat, I have been looking for you for some time. You are not so lively as you used to be. Are you feeling your age? You look worried. Pray tell me what is the trouble," said the officer as Pat entered the office.

"I have no trouble. I am wondering how a man feels that don't have to work or have any trouble."

"I don't know, Pat. I never had such a job. I always had to work hard for my honest living."

"Then the gentleman that is called the gentleman is not honest?"

"Not all, Pat. It would not include all wealthy men, but it would close the bars around some of them.

"Yes, and after the bars is closed, it is hard to get away, isn't it? I was thinking what a — of a time a man would have to get out of town if he could get from behind the bars."

"Some prisoners have got away and were never found, and again, some were caught in the act of getting away."

"And the results, if caught?"

"Pat, are you thinking of helping someone away? I never before heard you talk this way."

"I am thinking of the past, if a fellow lost his job, and of the future, if he found another one better."

"Are you thinking of leaving here, Pat?"

"Not if anyone would know it, I'm not leaving here."

"You know, Pat, I have always esteemed you very highly, and I should be very much disappointed if I had to lose confidence in you."

"You would be glad to place confidence in me, wouldn't you?"

"I surely would place all the confidence in the world in you, and would trust you with all of the prisoners and feel as safe as if I were here myself."

"I would take care of them one at a time—no other way."

"I know you would, Pat. I feel confident you would now, after this talk with you."

"I'm glad you feel that way. I may never hurt your feelings more than once."

"We can always forgive once, Pat, and sometimes twice, but you know the old adage, 'The third time is the charm.'"

"They would be only two and the third time would not be here."

CHAPTER XIX
A Clear Conscience Better than Money

"I do not understand, Pat, what made Pearson confess so meekly. He could at least have pleaded innocent until his trial. You know sometimes things look dark, and then a criminal can get out of it."

"Perhaps he thinks he can get out of here."

"Well, we will not have his trial here and now, without judge or jury; so, Pat, you may go and see if all is right among your fellow-men."

"I wonder if he understood what I meant to tell him all the time—what I was going to do—when he said he could forgive once and twice, and the old adage. I just as good as told him it would be twice, two of us, and the third time not here, and that was the daughter; she is not here to help get away, so there is the whole thing in a nut-shell. And the blockhead did not get it."

"I think Pat thinks he will make his get-away with his prisoner, and be a gentleman. I'm sorry for Pat. Now I have a problem to solve within myself. Shall I let him go ahead and make his plans, or shall I stop him before he gets started, and save the poor Irishman from occupying cell No. 76? I believe I can gain some knowledge by being deaf to it all. He is surely a clever Irishman, and I will see what plans he will make to escape with his prisoner, and I may be gaining knowledge, but I could not do so by sitting on Pat's seat of knowledge, so I think I will not leave this office."

"I hope that I shall receive a reply in regard to the real murderer, and that he will be brought here. That will help to open the way to a clear discovery of all this plot.

"What! A knock? I do hope that I shall not find a lady there."

"Good morning, officer."

"Good morning, Mr. McHenry." The visitor was Mr. McHenry, junior. "What can I do for you?"

"I should like to talk with you in regard to your new prisoner, Mr. Pearson. My father brought me the news, and I am not doubting him, but I truly would be better satisfied if I heard it through someone else also. Father was in such a rage that I could not calm him enough to understand the circumstances. I should appreciate your explaining it all to me."

"My boy, I am very sorry to say that I have to do my duty and the rules here we must comply with. We are not allowed to give out any information in regard to our prisoners, except to the officials."

"I ask for only enough to understand. Do you not see that I am in trouble? Can not you help me? Do tell me that he is innocent. It means so much to me."

"My young friend, I understand the circumstances. I learned them through your father. I am sorry for you and for the daughter of this man, but I am powerless to do anything."

"Could I talk with him?"

"No; I am not allowed to permit any information to be obtained inside of these prison walls."

"I am sure that it would never be known. I would never divulge the secret."

"I have confidence in you, but I should not be obeying rules here, and I could not allow you the privilege under any circumstances."

"I shall have to go, as I am unable to learn anything. Oh! could I not see him, just for one short conversation?"

"I am sorry. I must repeat that I can not allow you your wish, so please do not insist. It makes me feel bad to know, as I do, your predicament, and to hear you plead. I can not help you. There, I would not do that! The guard is coming. It is not necessary to let him see you shedding tears, and I would rather you would go before he comes in."

"I will go. I thank you for your sympathy, and I am certain you would have granted my request if it had been in your power to do so."

"I would, certainly. Good-bye."

"Good day, sir."

"Well, now I am getting in deeper. Even the poor young man's heart is broken. Engaged to the belle of the city, and not allowed to marry on account of the misdeeds of her father. Poor boy! My heart did ache for him when he broke down and cried."

"Well, I am after coming back. Do you need me?"

"I don't think I do, Pat. I am looking for some very important news. Outside of that, I would let you take charge of the office and I would take a stroll through the prison. I get very tired, sitting here from morning until night, and I like to take a walk around the inside walls, now and then, for exercise."

"You may do so. I will watch the place. I will see that no one comes in."

"Will you see that no one goes out, Pat? That is what I am here for. Very few want to break in and many would like to break out."

"You are not thinking of any one in particular, are you?"

"Oh, no! Almost any one of the prisoners would walk out if he had the chance."

"If they did, I surely would walk out with them."

"We are not looking for trouble, Pat. It probably will come soon enough. Open the door. I thought I heard a rap."

"So, you did, and so did I."

It was a messenger-boy. The communication read:

"We have a prisoner here, a confessed murderer. Will leave for your place in the morning."

"All right, no answer," the superintendent called to the waiting messenger.

"I am so glad to receive this."

"Is that the looked-for message?"

"It is, and the self-confessed murderer will be here to-morrow evening. With him they will bring the papers releasing No. 78, Clarence Pearson, an innocent man. Do you know anything about this, Pat? You sit there and do not look alarmed or excited over anything I am telling you. I usually act so when I understand it all."

"Well, I have nothing to say. If I did, I would say it without you asking me to. If I am not wanted, I'll stroll around; or do you want me to keep house and you stroll around? It is nearly bed-time."

"No; I think I shall retire, as I have been somewhat worried to-day. I shall lock up at once, and try to get around early in the morning, Pat. We shall have a new man to take care of to-morrow."

"I'll do that, sir."

"Now Pat is gone, and he will no doubt go at once to 77 cell and tell Pearson all he has learned. I wanted him to know that the man is coming and the brother would be a free man. I think I had best get some more information, so I'll just drop around and rest a while in 76 cell and see what the plot will be, as Pearson must know that he will have his trial soon. I feel certain that the officials have been prolonging matters through pity for the family. Mr. McHenry was probably slow to take action because his son was engaged to Pearson's daughter. Of course, he would try to avoid scandal as much as possible. I'll probably find Pat busy with his prisoner, fixing up their plot, so I'll lock up here and step around. What? I see Pat's going in now. I must hurry to get the first of the plot."

"I'm here, me friend."

"I'm glad to see you, Pat. We must decide to-night upon some way to make our get-away from here."

"Yes, and if we are not careful, the brother will bate us out."

"Have you heard anything?"

"Have I? Well, I heard it all. The real murderer will be here to-morrow, and then what will they hold him for?"

"My brother?"

"Yes, your brother."

"We must be out of here before to-morrow comes. What can we do? Now, Pat, make your wits work fast."

"I am thinking, and the main thing I'm thinking about is the money to make the gentleman out of me. Where is the money?"

"Don't let that worry you, Pat. I have plenty."

"Well, if you have plenty, if you give your brother back his money, you would be out of here as soon as he would, and save all scandal, and he a poor man freed from here, wouldn't he keep his mouth shut if he could be made a gentleman out of?"

"Pat, you do not understand."

"Well, then, explain it to me so I can understand. Can you do it?"

"I have told you that you would never have to work any more and you could be wearing fine clothes all the rest of your life, have I not?"

"That you have, but does that make it so? I'd like to see a pile of greenbacks in front of me before I explain any further."

"You see I am here tied up and can not get away. How can I show you the money?"

"Well, me friend, what is better than a clear conscience? Do you think money and a gentleman could show you a better time?"

"Oh, yes! I would not let a conscientious mind prevent me from having a good time the rest of my life."

"Me friend, your money is not showing you a good time, and the rest of your life your conscience will hurt you, and the pity and shame you have brought on your family—and those beautiful daughters—their lives are ruined, all by yourself, your greediness for money. No, me friend, I think I would rather be a hard-working Irishman all the rest of me life and have a clear conscience.

"Pat, you are a coward. I thought you would help me out of here."

"I did not help you in here, and why should I help you out?"

"Do you mean to go back on all the arrangements we have talked over?"

"That is what I do. Now I'll be telling you."

"Tell me what made you change your mind and talk this way?"

"Because I heard someone talk the other way."

"You heard someone talk the other way?"

"Yes, I fully intended to be a gentleman and help you out of this prison, and I thought I would walk around and think it over and see how bad I wanted to be a gentleman, and I got tired and sit myself down in the comfortable chair in the hospital, and there I was thinking it over and I was trying to think if I wanted to be a gentleman all the rest of me life, and when I asked myself the question I heard the answer, and, faith, I never had me mind made up yet—I was going to think about it a while—and I listened, as if I was hearing someone talking, and behold! I did, and I looked around, and not a soul was in sight, and I asked another question, and I got the answer again, and I thought: 'If you know so much and can answer all of my questions, I'll be giving you a job.' And I had a regular conversation with them, and in the conversation I asked them how much money you had, and they told me not enough to get out of the trouble you was in, so I think you will need it all, and I had better not try to handle any of it for you."

"Who was this you were talking with that gave you all of this information?"

"Well, me friend, I don't know. I did not see anyone, but I surely did hear someone."

"What are you going to do—let me stay here and serve whatever time is given me?"

"Well, what have I got to do with getting you out?"

"Look here! I've got you now where you will have to get me out, or I will get you in here to occupy the next cell, 76."

"I hardly think! That is taken. The murderer that is coming to-morrow will have that."

"Well, I am going to get away from here before to-morrow. I shall report to the office, if you do not help me out, of your accepting a bribe, as you agreed to do, to assist me in getting away. And they will look at it this way: If you can be bought off, you would not be a competent man to have in here. And that means you would lose your job, and you would find it hard to get employment elsewhere, for your dishonesty would follow you wherever you went."

"Just as yours have done. And, me friend Pearson, I have not committed the crime yet, and now I know, I never shall, so you just as well keep your head shut, for I am now in a position where I might show you some favors that I will do; but I will never show you the way out of this place."

"I am doomed to die here! It will kill me to have sentence passed on me in court, and I am guilty, and it will be proved. Pat, won't you please help me out? I will do anything for you. I will give you my beautiful daughter Gertie, whom you so much admire."

"You are very kind. I am after seeing one young man in trouble because he is in love with one of your beautiful daughters, and I'll be after loving a girl whose dad is out. I won't have to come to the penitentiary to ask for his girl."

"Then you have decided to allow me to remain here, have you, Pat?"

"I'm not the court."

"You are not going to help me out?"

"I am not."

"You shall rue this day. I shall explain everything to the office tomorrow."

"I'll go, then, and let you think about it, so you will have a good story to tell. Good night, Pearson."

"So, Pat has weakened! I'll see how he talks in the morning. I feel certain that to-morrow the officials will take steps to bring Pearson to trial, and I know that with what proof we have—and he has also pleaded guilty in the presence of the officials themselves—he will be sentenced for a number of years. I must now return to the office. I think Pat is out of sight. The crisis will come to-morrow."

"Well, me friend is mad because I do not help him out of his trouble and help myself into trouble. I wonder where I heard that voice. I'm glad I heard it when I did, and not after I did the dirty work."

"My boy, I was following you all the time, and would not have allowed you to commit the crime."

"What do I hear? Another voice, or is it the same? Well, me friend, I am a brave Irishman, and just as long as you want to talk to me you may do so. I'll sit here the rest of the night, and I won't have long to wait. It's nearly morning now. But I would of lost many a night's sleep, perhaps, if you had not of told me. Whoever you are—I don't know."

"And I am not going to tell you, now."

"I heard the words: 'I am not going to tell you, now.' I must be after getting out of this, for I'm hearing things, I am. I wonder if that strange voice has returned. I thought they—whoever it was, or whatever it was—had gone, never to return, but I do believe they have come back."

"I think Pat will be around soon, and I will pretend that I have had a restless night, and that I will not go to bed at this late hour," thought the superintendent. "He will be thinking this over and will not get it off from his mind. I shall be anxious, for I have been worried very much in the last few weeks. Yes, here he comes.

"Good morning, Pat."

"I'm not feeling any too good, officer."

"What is wrong, Pat?"

"Well, I'm after telling you at once. I've got myself in the penitentiary."

"Of course; we're all in here, but not from force."

"And I never would be here by choice, but I'm deserving of punishment, and I wish you would give it to me unbeknown to anyone of the higher officials, and I would plead guilty."

"Pat, what is wrong? I never heard you talk so before."

"And I never did do so before."

"Have you committed a murder?"

"No, your honor. But I come near liberating a convict. You have not the confidence in me any more you once had, or never—"

"Well, I am sorry, for I had a friend in you—or, at least, I felt so."

"And now I'm friendless, a lone Irishman, and I will soon be a convict."

"You don't seem to want to tell me what is wrong, and I want to talk with Pearson to-day. The telephone always rings when I am talking.

"Hello! Yes. You want me to bring Pearson to the office and read to him the warrant which I shall receive this morning? In the mail? His day for trial is set? All right, sir; I will obey orders. Good-bye.

"Pat, you may bring Pearson in. I see the mail is here, or soon will be."

"May I ask of you one favor?"

"Yes. What is it, Pat?"

"If a fellow—scoundrel, I think, is the best name for me—should repent of a crime before it is committed and never was committed, would you or could you forgive him? Could they send one of them things you are looking for when the postman comes in? Could they send one of them after me to—"

"Yes, Pat, if you are self-confessed criminal of some deed you have committed, you surely would receive one of those warrants."

"Why didn't I die when I was a babe, instead of me poor mother, and she here in me shoes and I in hers?"

"You must bring Pearson in here. Here is the postman."

"I will, your honor.

"And now for the dirty work of me poor self to be found out. I could see the wrong in others, and could not see when I was tempted the wrong I was doing, and I, like those here who committed crimes, will have to pay the penalty for it. I do not like to see this man Pearson go to the office this morning, but that is the orders, and I must bring him in. Here I've been wandering along and thinking of me own case, so I 'most forgot what I was sent for. This is his cell, and he is fast asleep, but I must awake him and take him to the office at once.

"Say! you! here! wake up! I want to take you for a walk."

"I am not asleep. I was just resting."

"Very well; come along. Your presence is wanted."

"And your presence will be wanted too, some day, if you don't change your mind before we get to the office."

"I shall never change my mind, not after I was told as I was and given such good advice from some unseen force."

"I've been thinking how to tell the whole story, and you will regret the day you changed your mind."

"I may do so. Here we are. The office is waiting for us, so come along."

"I say, Pat, are you going to change your mind before we enter the office?"

"Well, Pat, what are you debating about? Come along here. Time is flying," said the superintendent.

To the prisoner he said: "You are under arrest. You have been here accused of obtaining money under false affidavit, and I shall have to say—Pearson, I regret very much to have to read this to you, but I am sworn to do my duty, and I have done so in this case, as I would do in all others. Your trial is set for one week from to-day.

"You may take him back, Pat."

"Your honor, I have something to say."

"What have you to say, Pearson?"

"I will ask you if you have ever noticed Pat acting strangely, as if he was in a deep study?"

"I don't know as I have noticed it. I have had so many things to think of in the last three or four months. I do not really know if I have been noticing Pat very much, as he is one of the guards whom I can trust among all of the prisoners. I think Pat is very reliable—a very reliable man to have here."

"If I ever get out of this. I will never do any more dishonest work, or even talk or think about it. I pray me poor mother may help me. Now, you never did anything for me here on earth, mother, come down from Heaven, if you are there, and help me, please do help me keep me reputation up in this Pearson case, in the eyes of the whole world. I now realize what it means for a boy to make his first mistake. He is ruined for life, and if all of the young men knew what I do now, they would never start to commit any crime."

"What are you doing, Pat? Mumbling to yourself? No one can understand those sounds."

"I understand what he is doing. He has himself just where I will be soon, locked up in this place."

"Oh, Mr. Pearson! you always had a grievance against Pat. I have never seen any cause for it—none at all, I say."

"You will have, after I have explained all."

"You may take him back, Pat. It will soon be time for the Southwest Limited to arrive. Due in a half-hour. Make haste."

He mused: "Pearson is one of those men who, after he has been caught, wants to catch everyone else, and he will tell all on poor old Pat. I am so sorry for him. His first mistake, and a bad one at that, but I hope Pearson will be enough of a gentleman not to make him suffer for it. His conscience will hurt him enough for his part. I always placed so much confidence in Pat. I am heartily sick of the whole affair. One man can commit a crime and drag others down with him. Here comes Pat. He looks tired and worried."

"Well, your honor, I am back after a hard time I had getting the officer into his cell."

"Pat, why should he say what he did? Have you had some trouble with him, that you did not tell me about?"

"Your question shall be answered, but not to-day, not to-day."

CHAPTER XX
The Murderer Arrives

"Here is our new prisoner, the self-confessed murderer, and Clarence Pearson will be released.

"Open the door, Pat."

"Good morning, sir. I have a prisoner for you."

"Very well. Please register, here."

"You will have to, for me. My wrists hurt so I am not able to hold a pen in my hand, to say nothing of writing."

"Your name is—"

"William Devenart."

"A very odd name you have, Mr. Devenart.

"Pat, you may take care of him. Give him his bath and shave and new suit, then return to the office with Clarence Pearson."

"You poor, unfortunate fellow, you come along with me. Tell me all about yourself. I'm a guard here, and will treat you nice if you treat yourself so; but I want to give you a tip: Do not disobey rules. It will be better for you. How long are you sentenced here for?"

"Life."

"My man! A life sentence, indeed! You will eat many a meal with us, and I am not sure but what I will ate some off the same table."

"Do the guards and prisoners all eat together?"

"No, not always; but sometimes the guards turns into prisoners."

"I do not understand you."

"I do not know what I did mane, to do what I did. Here is the place. Clean yourself up and don the new suit, and very seldom do the styles change—I believe once in ten years, from stripes to checks. You will feel cool after you have been shaved and have a hair-cut. One advantage, you'll not be needing a comb very soon."

"Don't they allow you to comb your hair?"

"Oh, yes; but you don't have any to comb."

"Going to cut my hair off?"

"Sure, Mike—do all of 'me. And won't I be a peach if I have to get me own hair cut?

"The poor boy don't look like a criminal. I will be kind to him. I could see tears in his eyes when he was talking. If all of the young men could see some of these heart-rending cases, I do feel we would have less crime."

"What! A lady coming here? I do believe it is."

"Mrs. Pearson, come in," said the superintendent. "How do you do, Mrs. Pearson?"

"Good morning. I should like to see Mr. Pearson."

"Your husband?"

"No, sir; I have disowned him, but I want to talk with him. I have some papers I want him to sign. I also have an order from Mr.

McHenry allowing me to see him, as your rules could not be broken to accommodate anyone."

"No, madam, I could not break the rules, but with this order I can let you see him. I'll ring for a guard to bring him."

"I am to have a private conversation with him."

"I can not allow that, madam. You must say what you have to say in my presence, in this office."

"You are one of the most accommodating men, I must say, that I ever saw."

"I am sorry, very. I have heard you express your opinion of me, but I am here to do my duty, and will at all events. Here comes the guard. I will have your husband brought in at once.

"Bring the prisoner from cell 77."

"Oh dear! You have him locked up, and call for him by his number, do you? And he has not had a trial, nor has he been convicted of any crime."

"We have a warrant for his arrest. His trial will be this week. I hope that he will be able to prove his innocence. I am very sorry for him. I have grieved over the matter considerably."

"Well, I have not grieved at all. I am going to disown him after I get his signature. Then I shall have all the property in my own name, and I shall try to forget that I ever had a husband—a criminal. My daughter Amelia will be married one week from to-day, and we can not be disgraced by coming here after the marriage takes place, and that is why I am here to-day. Is that he coming?"

"No; I have a prisoner who is to receive his freedom, and that is Pat, bringing him in. By the way, that is your brother-in-law."

"How dare you insult me in that way? I acknowledge a criminal as a relative? No, never!"

"Well, here is your 'fellow,' No. 78. I can't say 'prisoner' any longer. He gets his freedom to-day, and me old shoes will have to go with him, for I don't think I can get them to track any other direction after the prisoner 78 is gone out. Have you sent for the officer convict? Here he comes."

"Yes, Pat. Don't you see Mrs. Pearson sitting there?"

"I beg your pardon, madam. I very seldom see a lady."

"All brutes of men are alike."

"Pearson, you may come in. Your wife is here to see you, and you may be seated over there. I will look after your brother, here. He gets his freedom to-day. The real murderer is in his new suit, and will be given his occupation in the morning."

"Did I hear that I am a free man?"

"You are, Clarence. Here are the papers."

"And my brother? Oh! what will you do with him? Turn him loose?"

"No; not until we hear from the court. He will have his trial this week, and I hope we will then be able to turn him loose."

Mrs. Pearson addressed her husband as he approached her: "I want you to sign over all of your part and interest in this home we, your daughters and I, occupy. I will not live under a roof owned by a criminal, and you shall be disowned at once. I have already made application—before my daughter is married, I shall have all ties broken with you."

"I am not going to sign over any of the property. It is not mine at all. It belongs to my brother here. I spent and lost all of my estate, and that is why I am here to-day. I swore that he was dead and, in that way, got his share, and what we now have is his. He is alive and free, and he is innocent, and here am I, a criminal and guilty, and bound down here for no one knows how long."

"Oh, dear brother! is this your wife? And she spoke of your daughters. You have not told me anything about them. I can not see you separated from them all for the loss of my money. What would I do with it, now, to know that I would cause so much misery to obtain it? I could not be happy. Oh, if I could only step in your shoes and you in mine! I would gladly do so. And you, my dear sister-in-law, how sorry I am to know that this has happened!"

"If you had never committed a murder—you, I say—feigning mercy for your brother, we would not have to suffer."

"I am not a murderer. Here are my papers of freedom, and the real murderer is here in my place—self-confessed, and he will be punished for the crime. If my dear brother could only be found as innocent as I am, you would have your beautiful home always. As it is, I shall claim what is due me, and what was left me by the will of my dear mother."

"You may have a hard time to get it."

"I am willing to turn all over to my brother. He is entitled to it, and it belongs to him," said the husband.

"Get some water, Pat. Mrs. Pearson has fainted."

As she revived Mrs. Pearson asked that a carriage be called.

The superintendent replied: "You may step into this room. I will call one.

"Mr. Pearson, you may return to your cell. Pat, take him back to 77."

"Oh, brother! what can I do for you?"

"Pray for me. You got me here. Except for you, I would be a free man."

"Clarence, you may sign here. Here are the papers of freedom. I want to shake hands with you. I hope that you will never again be placed in such a position," said the superintendent.

"I thank you, sir. I am under obligations to you for many favors, and I hope that you will always be as just to all the other prisoners as you have been to me."

"I shall try to be. Good-bye."

"Good-bye, sir."

"Your carriage is here, Mrs. Pearson."

"Good-bye, officer."

"Good-bye, madam."

"Drive to 1715 North Twenty-third Street," said Mrs. Pearson.

CHAPTER XXI
REMORSE

"Now, Clarence has his freedom and has left the prison. Next comes the trial of the officer, and poor Pat, what a predicament he is in! I must have him for a witness in this case. I must try to find out all he knows, and if it will not assist any in the Pearson case, I will try to get along without him. Well, I thought Pat just stepped out to avoid the Pearson scene. I hope that he will return soon. I shall have to notify the officials of the new prisoner's arrival. Here comes Pat.

"Well, Pat, I thought you had walked away with Clarence Pearson. The poor fellow was a happy man when he left this place."

"They will have the same thing to say when someone else walks away from here."

"Pat, I did not say 'they'; I said 'I.' To whom are you alluding as 'they,' and when who walks away?"

"Well, your honor, I am the next to give the papers to, and please give me my papers of resignment. I don't believe I want the job any longer. I am not after looking for a long job here."

"It is bed-time now, Pat. To-morrow will bring forth something new. Pearson's trial will take place, and probably you may have to fill his office, as assistant, here with me. We shall have to have another man in his place. I think you could do it."

"Yes, I could probably fill the place he is now about to fill. I am not looking for the job, indeed I am not."

"Pat, you are worried to-night. So much excitement the last three or four months has upset you. It will have to be settled—all will be settled after Pearson gets located, and now it is late, and we must retire. Good night."

"Good night, officer."

Pat muttered: "As I hear the big iron door slam after me it makes me blood run cold. I am in a fix. What is money for? To make criminals, I believe. I believe every convict under this blooming roof is here for or on account of money. The vile stuff! We get a living, and have to work, or should if we don't, and it only keeps us out of mischief—and then it don't. I am in it now, and I have been working too, but there it leads up to money, for the fine clothes and the gentleman, and the good times that would go with it. I would be able to go and lay me head down on me pillow to-night and slape if it wasn't for money. Instead of that, I have to pace around this place all the night. Yes, here it is nearly morning, and not a wink of slape. I'd just as soon be guilty, as so near and not, for I am taking on the same guilty condition. I believe I'll walk around and see if me friend is worrying over me as much as I am myself. What? I hear him talking to the new prisoner. I'll see if he is telling him how to behave himself. I don't believe they placed the new man in 78—yes, indeed, they did. I remember, he said the real murderer would be occupying Clarence's cell and Clarence would have his freedom. Well, he is talking very nice to the new man. I will see what the conversation is about."

"Tell me about it," said Pearson. "How did you come to confess that you were the real murderer of this woman? They had a man serving time for the crime."

"Yes; that is why I confessed, and for other reasons."

"What were the other reasons? Would you mind telling me?"

"I am trying to forget it. I will tell you, and then I shall never repeat it again. It is too horrid; I can not stand it to talk about it. I was married only a short time, and a difference arose, one day, between my dear wife and myself. I became angry, and was talking loudly, when the door opened and this fellow who was serving time here for the crime came rushing in unannounced, and asked my wife if he could assist her. She was afraid of me, but she declined to accept his help. He left with apologies for intruding. I grew more excited, and in a fit of uncontrollable temper I choked her to death. I came to myself and found her lying at my feet dead. Oh, man! can you picture the agony I was in? I thought of that man, and how I could lay the murder on him. I ran from the house and met an officer. I told him my wife was just murdered by a man whom I had just seen leave the house. The officer rushed up the street, and I recognized the man as the same who had offered to help my poor wife, and I shouted, 'There he is!' and to jail the officer took him. At the trial I swore that he was the murderer, knowing that I myself was the guilty one, and he was the man who was given his freedom to-day. I will tell you all, as I have started. I know that all the time he was here I suffered more than he ever could."

"In what way, Devenart?—is that your name?"

"Yes; but just call me 'Will.' I do not want to disgrace my father and mother by causing their name to be spoken.

"I can not tell you in what way. I can tell you the mysterious way I was punished. I never lay down and closed my eyes that I did not see my poor dead wife, and presently another woman would come up to me and point her finger at me with scorn. After many terrible nights, I began to hear noises. I could not at first understand, and one night I was touched by some unknown hand, and I was frightened beyond words. I thought, 'If I could only die and get away from it all!' I am so excited now I can not talk longer."

"I should like to have you finish. We may not get a chance again, as you know the rules are, 'No talking among the prisoners.'"

"I am glad that I have rested to-night without seeing her face, and I will never tell the story again. As I am here for life, I know that I never shall, if we can not talk.

"One night, as I was sitting on the side of my bed, I could not lie down and close my eyes, and I saw my wife walk up to me, and by her side came an elderly lady, and I tried to close my eyes so I could not see them, but I could see them as plainly with my eyes closed as with them open. I stood up and begged them to go away and let me rest for the remainder of the night. Then, for the first time, I heard a voice, and it was the motherly lady who spoke, and these were her words—oh! I am telling the terrible story under a dreadful strain; I am living it all over again. I thought I saw the same lady standing by your side, as I am looking through these bars."

"You will have strength, I hope, to tell me all. Please finish the story."

"I will finish now, if I am—oh, she spoke to me! Was that where I left off? I believe it was. The elderly lady came closer than my poor wife did, and as she spoke, I can never explain the feelings I had. I called for help. I prayed and fell down on my knees and asked for mercy and help. The voice answered:

"'So did your wife pray for her life, and it was not spared—by the hands of a brute, and that was you. Now you suffer as you have caused her to suffer—I say suffer!'

"My friend, can you think of a punishment like that? I could bear punishment from the hands of my fellow-men, but when I know not from whence it comes or what it is, it is terrible. I am suffering for all the sins I ever committed.

"My man, I see, I do see, the same lady by your side, and my wife!

"O Father, come to me in this hour of need. I am being punished for the terrible crime I have committed. May I not be shown mercy? I am guilty, and have pleaded so, and will plead guilty, even in my prayers to Thee. Help and forgive me. How I have suffered! Thou knowest, and Thou alone. From this on I shall live as I should—pray every day for the forgiveness of my sins. Each day will I pray for guidance and help in all my undertakings. Help me to live the way I should live. Turn not a deaf ear to me, O Father. I am in sorrow and need Thy help. I am here that the one who has received his freedom may go forth with Thy blessing; that the whole world may look on him as an innocent man, and not as a murderer, as I swore that he was. I ask also for help for him. May he forgive me. I may never have the opportunity to meet him on this earth, but I hope to meet him in Heaven, as innocent of all crime as he was of that of which I accused him. O blessed Father, I do feel that Thou wilt answer my prayers. Amen!"

"Well, well, you can pray as well as murder," said Pearson. "I was wondering if you ever prayed before."

"No, my friend, and if you would experience the heavy burden lifted from your shoulders as I did from that prayer, you would pray, or try to, as I did."

"I think I had better get away from here, if they are going to have prayer-meeting," muttered Pat. "I wonder if a bit of a prayer would do me good. The first chance I get, I believe I will do a little of it. Well, here is another day, and nearly time for the trial. I had better step in the office a bit."

"Pat, your absence this morning makes me think you had a good night's rest."

"I will call it rest when I get it. Indeed, I never closed me eyes."

"Was anything wrong with the prisoners? I was going to ask you to go by cell 78 and see our new prisoner, and it passed from my mind."

"I did the very thing that passed from your mind. I guess it came to my mind."

"Is everything all right?"

"Yes. We had some prayers, and I think it helped the fellow that prayed, and I am thinking of doing a little of it myself, when I get a chance."

"The poor man! Remorse always sets in after they get in behind the bars, Pat. Do you know that this is a hard place to be—to work for a livelihood? You have no trouble of your own, but you worry about the other fellow's trouble."

"Faith, and if I had no troubles of me own, I would let the other fellow worry about his own."

"You have no troubles to worry over. See how long you have been here, and you could not get into trouble here, could you?"

"No, I couldn't, but I have."

"You have? Tell me, Pat, what is wrong."

"We had better put that off."

"It will soon be time for Pearson's trial, and you will be one of the witnesses. As he has confessed that he is guilty, I think it will go hard with him."

"Now, me friend, your honor, I'm not going to keep the secret any longer. I just as well have it out with, and you may cut down expenses and have two trials at once. I have a secret to tell you. Every bit of it is the truth, and I too am going to confess, and then, when I get the chance, I'll pray, and perhaps I too will feel better."

"Go ahead, Pat."

"I am after listening, and I heard the man to be tried to-day trying to spend five thousand dollars easy, and I thought: 'If you have it to give away, I myself would take a little of it.' And I in a way as much as told him so, and then I changed me mind. I thought I would like this job the best. Now he insists I spend his money, and I don't want it at all, and I told him so. Now he has threatened to turn me over to the officials here if I don't be a gentleman, and I never was one, and now I know I couldn't be one, so there is the secret."

"Well, we must now attend court. You will have to tell all you know, Pat. You may go for Pearson and take him to court. I will be there presently."

"Here is me punishment beginning now. I am after getting a taste of it myself. I may be the next poor devil to court. For the love of Mike! what will I do? Pray? I haven't the time now. I will after I get through with this trial, and then I may have something to pray for. Here I am at the cell, and I believe he's asleep. Now, I wonder if he was awake all night. I'm not asleep, and I was up too, all night. I will get him out of here."

"Come, Officer Pearson! Your trial is at hand, and I have come for you."

"I'm willing to go, Pat—and say, Pat, are you for me, or against me?"

"I am neither, if I don't have to be."

"If you are called to the stand, what will you say—anything about our plot to get away?"

"Will you say anything about it if I am not called to the stand?"

"I'm not quite sure if I will or not, Pat. I must be out of here, and if you will get me out, I will not mention anything about your offering to liberate me."

"If you think you can get away without my help, you may do so—if I don't see you; but if I see you, you won't get away. Here we are at the court."

CHAPTER XXII
Pat's Testimony

"You are taking your time, Pat. We are waiting for you."

When court had been opened and the preliminaries had been gone through, Mr. Pearson was examined.

"You are registered under your correct name, are you not?"

"I am."

"Mr. Pearson, how long has your mother been dead?"

"Twenty-one years."

"Did she leave a will?"

"Yes, sir."

"Did you know that you were the only heir?"

"No, sir—well, I thought so."

"But you did not know for sure?"

"No, sir."

"Mr. Pearson, did you take oath that you knew your brother was dead?"

"I did; yes, sir. I thought he was. We had never heard from him."

"Did you look for him, or try to find him?"

"Well, no."

"Did you acknowledge him as a brother when you did find him?"

"I did."

"Not until you had to."

"Well, I tried to do for him after I found him."

"In what way?"

"I told him I would help him."

"Out of prison, or financially?"

"Well, I don't know,"

"You don't know what you were going to do, but you were going to do something for him?"

"I felt that I should."

"Will you tell the court what you were going to do, or thought of doing? Now, Mr. Pearson, you have been holding a position of authority, have you not?"

"Yes, sir."

"Have you done an officer's duty?"

"I have tried to."

"You tried to, but did you?"

"I don't know."

"You are excused."

Pat was called to the stand.

"Your name?"

"Me name is Pat Dugan."

"Well, Pat, what do you know about this Officer Pearson?"

"Your honor, I wish I had never seen the man."

"That is not answering my question."

"Well, I don't know what he did all the time, but I know I wish I did not know what he did any of the time."

"Answer the question."

"Please repeat it, I am after forgetting the question."

"Tell what you know in regard to this case. Did Officer Pearson fill his position as an officer should?"

"Now, me friend, I don't think that is the same question at all."

"Well, answer it, if you do or don't think the question was worded just the same."

"I did not hear the last question. I was thinking of how to answer the first one. Now, me friend, I will ask you to repeat the last once more, and I might answer them both."

"I suppose we must have patience with you, for I don't think you were ever in court before, and I know it is hard for you. Now, once more, I ask you about Officer Pearson's conduct as an officer. That is a short question and you should be able to answer it without hesitation."

"I will say that I think the job is a hard one for me, and I will give you my club and quit at once."

"Sit down, Pat! Sit down there and answer these questions the attorney is asking you, or I shall fine you for contempt of court."

"Could I get off—out of that fine for contempt of court—as if I told the truth?"

"I am asking you a question now, and I wish you would answer."

"Faith, and you have been asking me some questions I didn't know how to answer, and I am only an ignorant Irishman, and you are one of the know-alls, or should be. I've always thought that if anything ever came up with a business consideration, 'I will ask me lawyer about that.' This is the first time I have ever been smart enough to talk to one of them lawyers."

"Well, you are taking your time to talk. You must like our company."

"I like to hear a smart man talk; indeed, I do."

"Well, the court would like to know if this is a trial, or a complimentary case."

"Your honor, I am trying to get the witness to answer my questions."

"Put the question to him again."

"Now pay attention, Pat, and we will soon be through with you."

"Couldn't you turn me loose now? I am feeling sick, me man. I am sick."

"Get him a drink.

"Here is water. Take this, Pat. Drink some water. You are all right now."

"You know everything in the books, but you don't know how a fellow feels inside, and please don't talk to me—please don't. I wonder, if I would pray, would I feel better? I am going to pray, gentlemen. I believe me time has come right now.

"O Father in Heaven, if You ever send blessings to the Irish, send this one Irishman some now. I need it. O me God, I did not do anything. I changed me mind before I let him go, and he is here, and You can do as You please with him. I am through with him. I think You will know what he needs, and give it to him. Have mercy on me, and him too, if he is deserving of it. I don't think he is, but Your judgment is best, and use it, and be sure You use good judgment in my case, and help me out of this terrible predicament, and if I never get in another, I won't pray any more. You will see I am in earnest and don't delay the job. I am awfully sick, but I think I feel better now, and if the court will have mercy on me, and You do likewise, I know I will be well in a few minutes. Help Your wandering one all alone in this country. Me poor mother has been with You a long time, and if I was there too, I would not be here, in this fix. And now I have prayed for the first time in all me life, and if You don't answer, I shall say my prayers were all in vain; but if You will let me know that they were heard, I will let you hear them again, if I get in trouble. Amen."

"The judge spoke: 'Stand up, Pat. You are good on praying, and you have a nice way of doing it, if you did convict yourself. Go. I don't think your crime is punishable, and I want to give you some orders. You had better learn to pray now, and do some of it. Don't wait until you are in trouble and then ask the Lord to help you. Serve Him all the time, and you will then be guided, so you will not have to ask for help in time of trouble. Too many wayward boys like you, Pat, get in trouble before they ever think of praying. I hope that the Father to whom you prayed has heard your prayers. I feel that He did, and that is why I am going to turn you loose; so, you may say your prayers were not in vain, but go from this court-room with prayers on your lips, and pray often. It will do you good. Now you may go, and may God bless you.'

"Well, if I ever get me another job, I will never get it in a prison—I may not get out so easy next time; but the poor man, he is there yet, and I never told a word of his trying to give me all his money and fine clothes.

"Well, I'll be willing to work, now, for all I get. And I'll say to myself: 'Didn't the man who was boss of the job make a fine speech to me?' He must know nearly as much as the lawyer did, and I felt sorry for him when he felt sorry for me and told me to pray. Faith, and I will pray, and I will keep it up as long as I live, and after I am dead, I will come back and scare some of the poor devils and make them pray like the new man. Oh, how he did pray when he thought he saw the dead woman! And it was that very thing got me started to praying, and only for that I believe they would of hanged me this very day of me life."

"Well, here I am back to the office, and I have me clothes all here, and I want to bid me old friend good-bye before I go. I can't keep the tears back. I guess I am feeling pretty bad again. I believe I'll just step in here and pray to myself now, while I'm waiting for me old friend that thought so much of me."

In the court-room the trial proceeded. At length the judge arose, saying:

"I am not of the opinion that a crime of as long standing as this one is punishable in the eyes of the law. Twenty-one years would outlaw it. If the prisoner will give his penniless brother a home for life, I will set him free.

"What have you to say to that, Pearson? Are you willing to share your home with your brother?"

"I thank your honor. I am more than willing, and I will see that he shares my home as a brother should, without feeling under obligations."

"Pearson, I feel that you mean all right, and I will ask you to let me hear from you as soon as you find your unfortunate brother who was freed several days ago. I want you to help him to live down the disgrace of his long imprisonment, and live as brothers should. We have all learned to pray through this unfortunate affair, or we should have learned, and that not waiting until we are in trouble, and then expect our prayers to be heard, but we have learned to pray at all times—not as Pat did, if we get help, say we won't pray any more until the next time we are in trouble."

Later, when Pearson appeared at the office, he said: "Officer, I am discharged from all, including my position, am I?"

"Well, Pearson, we have been holding consultation in the side room—the officials and I, and we have decided to reinstate you, and Pat also. We have decided that this lesson will make honest men out of you and Pat, and trusty. You did not betray Pat and he did not betray you. It was a good principle that you both showed this morning, and we feel that you will work hand in hand together in the future. I wonder if Pat has gone. We will step over to his room and see."

"I hope that Pat will feel kindly toward me. I have forgotten all, and will always remember that trial—how poor Pat feigned sickness to avoid answering those questions. Poor old Pat! He is a good Irishman."

"I do believe that he is gone. This is his room, is it not?"

"Yes. Here he has left a note. He has written: 'Good-bye to all the poor fellows in here. I have served me term and am ready to go, but with tears. I am thinking I am all alone, save God. He is ever near me. Good-bye to all fellow-men!'"

CHAPTER XXIII
Prayer-Meeting in Prison

"That is the first time I have seen you break down."

"Yes, Pearson, I am heart-broken. I shall never forget Pat, not for the sickness he feigned, but for the feeling that came over me when he was praying. I have never prayed, but I am going to this day. And the very next Sabbath I am going to start a prayer-meeting in this prison. If it helps all as much as it did Pat, I will feel repaid for all these mysterious voices and visions which we have heard and seen here. Besides, it may lift up many a sad heart inside these walls, that could get no help except through prayer."

"You locked the door as you left the office, did you?"

"Only the outside door."

"I see bundles in there. They belong to Pat. He has not gone."

"Take a look into the room next the office, Pearson."

"Oh, my God!"

"What? suicide?"

"No; praying."

"Pearson, close the door."

"I am after being through and I feel better. I have been praying to me Father to help me find another job, or to get this one back for me."

"Pat, your prayer is answered, once again. You may remain and do as you have done. Outside of this little trouble, you have been a good, faithful man, and I feel that you and Officer Pearson will from this day on be faithful to the trust which is imposed in you, and that you will show brotherly love and kindness toward each other and all your fellow-men. I want you to be sure to be at prayer-meeting Sunday morning, and open the meeting with prayer.

"I shall expect you, Pearson, to close the meeting with prayer. I will take a hand at it myself, and I hope that we may hear the voices of all in this prison, asking for help and guidance and peace.

"Now, Pat, see that all is right.

"Well, Pearson, I am glad to see you sitting there under different circumstances, and I hope this will be a lesson for us all. Honesty is always the best policy. If you follow that precept, you will never get into trouble," said the superintendent, addressing Mr. Pearson.

"Well, here is one good Irishman the rest of me life, and I will be after being a Sunday-school teacher; I think that would bate being a gentleman any time. And now I'll see if the officer has not forgot to put the poor man that was brought in to work. Forgot? I know he did. I'll be after going and asking where will I take the poor fellow to work, and I'll ask mercy for him, for it means a job for life with him, poor fellow. I am after passing the knowledge-seat. I will walk in and tell me business at once. I got enough knowledge to do me at that resting-place.

"What do I see? The poor fellow that was turned out of here sitting in the office? I will pretend not to know him, and make my business be known and lave at once.

"Officer!"

"Yes. What is it, Pat?"

"You have been after forgetting to give the poor man his life job."

"So, I have, Pat. I will find a place in a trade where he will not have to toil so hard, for it means a long time for him. I will take care of that Monday morning, Pat. Don't bother him. Let him get used to his new clothes and room. You may go, Pat. I'll take care of him Monday."

"So, you have come back to see us, have you, Clarence?"

"Yes, officer. I could not rest and know that my brother was here in prison, all on my account. I am the cause of it all. I should have written home after I left. I should have written to my dear mother. Then I could have been notified when she died, and poor Oliver would not be in this trouble. That is why I am taking all this disgrace upon myself.

"Brother, I am going to help you, but not in the way I asked you to be helped at first. I am going to take you home now, and introduce you to my family, and try to have a family reunion, in honor of the prodigal son's return—in honor of poor mother."

"You may go now, Mr. Pearson. I can spare you for a few hours."

"Come along, brother. Clasp my hand and we will walk hand in hand to my home—or, rather, yours, and we will spend the rest of our days together."

"Oh, how beautiful your voice sounds to me, Oliver! As I walk along by your side I feel as if we were indeed beginning a new life."

"By the way, we shall have a wedding soon. My daughter Amelia is to be married to-night, at ten o'clock—yes. And we shall be there on time, I see. The place is all aglow. I wonder—"

"Yes, and I wonder how I will be received."

"You must be treated as my brother, and the family will do so. Music? Yes, Gertie, playing 'Home, Sweet Home.' There is no place like home. Oh, how true! We will surprise them. Just step in, Clarence."

"Oh, papa, papa!"

"Yes, Gertie; I heard you playing just as I feel, that there is no place like home."

"Mother, see who is here."

"My dear wife, I want you to meet my brother, as a gentleman—which he is, and has been proved to be.

"And, Clarence, this is Gertie, my pet now, as I must soon give Amelia to someone else.

"I hope that he will be as kind to you, Amelia, as your father has always been."

www.ingramcontent.com/pod-product-compliance
Lightning Source LLC
Chambersburg PA
CBHW020906080526
44589CB00011B/460